Vacuuming in the NUDE

AND OTHER WAYS TO GET ATTENTION

PEGGY ROWE

Foreword by MIKE ROWE

Forefront
BOOKS

Vacuuming in the Nude
And Other Ways to Get Attention

Copyright © 2022 by Peggy Rowe

Published by Forefront Books.

Print ISBN: 978-1-63763-099-0
E-book ISBN: 978-1-63763-100-3

Library of Congress Control Number: 2022909300

Cover Design by Bruce Gore, Gore Studio, Inc.
Cover Illustration by Jaime Buckley
Interior Design by Bill Kersey, KerseyGraphics

To John Rowe, who knew that I was a writer long before I did. And who had the courage to call me one—in public—even before I was published.

"In everyone's life, at some time, our inner fire goes out. It is then burst into flame by an encounter with another human being."
~ALBERT SCHWEITZER

CONTENTS

FOREWORD

THIS IS MY MOTHER'S THIRD BOOK, AND IT IS, without question, her best.

Conversely, this is my third foreword, and it is, without question, my worst.

The problem with this foreword began in May 2018 with a phone call from my mother, while I was filming an episode of *Somebody's Gotta Do It.*

"Michael, I'm sorry to interrupt your shoot, but when you have a few moments, would you mind writing the foreword for my first book?"

"Of course, Mom! It would be an honor."

My mom's first book was a warm and funny collection of short stories about her mother, ingeniously titled *About My Mother.*

"I know you're busy," she said, "but the publisher says a foreword from a celebrity will boost sales, and you're the only celebrity I know."

I canceled my dinner plans that evening, went back to my hotel, and stayed up until 4 a.m. writing the best foreword I could possibly write. I mean, really, how could I say no? When your eighty-year-old mother asks you to write the foreword for her first book, you have to consider the possibility that it might also be the foreword for her *last* book. And so, I left nothing on the table. I not only raved about my mother's persistence and determination, I shared some of my own stories about Nana and offered a few observations on the remarkable mother-daughter relationship she and my mother shared for sixty-seven years. Modesty aside, it was a foreword fit for a *New York Times* best-seller, which is exactly what *About My Mother* became the day it hit the shelves.

Naturally, I was thrilled for my mom, but I was surprised by the call I received two years later while filming an episode of *Returning the Favor*.

"Michael, I'm sorry to interrupt your shoot, but when you have a few moments, would you mind writing the foreword for my second book?"

My mom's second book was a warm and funny collection of short stories about my father, ingeniously titled *About Your Father*.

"Well, Mom, to be honest, my last foreword was pretty thorough. I'm not sure what I can say that I haven't said already."

"I know, Michael, but you have such a way with words. Just a few lines, dear, when you have a moment."

"What about Dad? He's got a way with words too."

"Your father's a very busy man, Michael. And besides, you're still the only celebrity I know...."

I canceled my dinner plans that evening, went back to my hotel, and stayed up until 4 a.m., writing the best foreword I could possibly write. I mean, really, how could I say no? When your eighty-two-year-old mother asks you to write the foreword for her second book, you can't help but consider the possibility that it might also be her *last* book. And so, once again, I held nothing back. I not only raved about her persistence, determination, and natural talent, I also shared a few funny stories about my dad and the many delightful idiosyncrasies that have endeared him to so many people. Now, was my second foreword as good as my first foreword? No. The sequel is never as good as the original. But apparently, it was good enough for another *New York Times* best-seller, which is exactly what *About Your Father* became the moment it hit the shelves.

Once again, I was thrilled by my mother's success, but surprised by the phone call I received two years later, while filming a new episode of *Dirty Jobs*.

"Michael, I'm sorry to interrupt your shoot, but when you have a few moments, would you mind writing the foreword for my third book?"

"You gotta be shitting me."

"Michael! Language!"

"Sorry, Mom. I'm in a septic tank. Can I call you back this evening?"

"Of course, dear. But the publisher is in a terrible hurry. Do you think we could get a foreword from you sometime tomorrow?"

Again, how could I say no? If there's one thing I've learned about the entertainment business, it's never to turn your back on a winning formula. (Why else would I still be hosting a TV show from a septic tank?) And now, at eighty-four years of age, my mother's discovered the same is true in publishing. And so, here I am once again, sitting in a hotel at 1 a.m., searching for something new to share about my mother's lifelong obsession with the written word. Something I haven't already told you twice.

Okay, how about this?

When I was baby, my mother used to write stories while she was nursing me. I don't remember this, thank

God, but Mom told me recently that I nearly choked to death one morning because she had left me "latched on" to the point where I could no longer swallow. Apparently, she was so immersed in whatever she was writing, she forgot about the baby on her boob, swelling up like a tick.

That's the essence of the woman on the cover of this book. An aspiring author who never stopped writing. A distracted housewife who imagined herself a best-selling author, sixty years before she became one.

For as long as I can remember, my mother has been armed with a yellow legal pad and a #2 pencil, chronicling the world around her. To this day, she still writes everywhere she goes. Beauty salons, baseball games, state fairs, supermarkets, pool halls, and planetariums . . . you never know where she'll whip out her yellow pad and start scribbling. Whereas my father still enters a bathroom with a book or a newspaper, my mother goes in with her pad and pencil and comes out with a screenplay or a sonnet.

"You never know when inspiration might strike," she says. "Or when you'll see something worth jotting down."

My mother loves her three sons, but growing up, she never really talked to us—she interviewed us. When I came home from my first summer camp in 1975, she was waiting for me at the kitchen table with her pad and pencil.

"Welcome home," she said. "I missed you. Now, tell me everything. Leave nothing out."

I told her how much I had loved the woods, the wildlife, and the nightly campfires. I told her about canoeing down the rapids, winning the archery competition, and sleeping under the stars. The faster I talked, the faster she scribbled. I told her about navigating with a map and compass and cooking the fish I caught myself in a mountain stream. I told her about the bear that raided our camp and ate all our food and the hot air balloon ride that nearly ended in disaster when we missed power lines by inches before landing in a tree. Two days later, there was a story on my pillow called "A Dangerous Walk in the Woods," with a daring young protagonist whose adventures were identical to my own.

In December of that year, my father decided it would be foolish to buy another Christmas tree.

"Why pay good money for a tree" he asked, "when the woods out back are full of them?"

So my dad fired up the tractor, loaded the cart with axes and saws, and led my brothers and me on a quest to find the perfect Christmas tree. What we brought home, however, was not a fir, a pine, or a spruce. Honestly, I don't know what it was. It looked like a hedge with a pointy top, and it took up half of our living room.

I remember mom scribbling away as my brothers and I were stringing lights and hanging tinsel. I recall Christmas carols playing on the transistor radio and the aroma of gingerbread wafting in from the kitchen. My dad was trying to affix the star to the top of our pointy hedge when suddenly, a starling flew out from the tangled depths and bounced off his forehead. I remember my brothers and me laughing as our dog took off after the bird, barking like mad and chasing it all over the house. Mostly though, I remember the script that appeared beneath the tree on Christmas morning—an elaborate radio play that chronicled the events of that day with individual roles for everyone in the family. Later that day, we recorded "A Christmas for the Birds" by Peggy Rowe on a newfangled reel-to-reel tape recorder, liberated from the AV department of the junior high school where my father taught. I'm pretty sure she still has that tape.

It was her fundamental inability to distinguish between "life" and "material" that compelled my mother to write. To her way of thinking, everything was content, and everyone fair game for a future story—including the dearly departed. I recall more than a few funerals when my mother was called upon to deliver the eulogy and left the mourners in stitches.

"It's fun to write for dead people," she says. "They're so much more appreciative than publishers."

She preferred to write about the living, however, and boy, did she. Every few days there was a new profile pinned to our refrigerator with a magnet. I recall the story about a cop who still patrolled the neighborhood on horseback, the crab fisherman who hadn't taken a day off in thirty years, and the old man who lived down that road who had been awarded the Silver Star for action at Iwo Jima.

Mom's stories often appeared in newspapers and magazines, but whenever she sent them off to a major publisher—with a proposal to turn them into a book—the only thing that came back was a rejection letter. There was just no appetite for a random collection of stories cobbled together by an unknown housewife in Baltimore. Unless you were my father, who preferred to read my mother's stories aloud, oftentimes to total strangers.

"Pardon me," he'd say, sliding into a crowded booth at Bob's Big Boy, "but I've got a treat that you folks won't find on the menu." He'd then pull a few pages from his back pocket and say, "Have you heard the latest from Peggy Rowe?"

Most people had no idea how to respond to this kind of unsolicited entertainment, so they simply sat there, perplexed, as a short man with a loud voice began to read my mother's latest poem, play, or short story. One day in a packed elevator, my father began reciting a series of limericks my mom had written that Sunday during the sermon.

"Pretty good, right? And she's not even Irish!"

And that's the way it was for sixty years.

Mom wrote hundreds of stories, the publishers rejected them all, and my father read them out loud to whoever would listen.

Imagine that if you can.

Six decades of, "Thank you for your submission, but not at this time."

Six decades of, "Hey, my wife wrote a haiku on a Ferris wheel. I'll read it for you!"

If you've read the forewords in either of my mother's previous bestsellers, you know that her first "publisher" was me. Back in May 2018, I printed 10,000 copies of *About My Mother* and offered them for sale on Facebook. Seemed the least I could do for the woman who nearly drowned me in breast milk. Those first ten thousand copies sold out in no time, and that got the attention of the big boys, who took a closer look at my mother's work; they finally realized what her husband had known all along—that Peggy Rowe is a hell of a writer. Which brings us to the book you're about to begin.

Vacuuming in the Nude is the true story of one writer's journey. It is not an attempt to teach you how to write or how to get published. And while it is a love letter to persistence and determination, it's not a blanket invitation to "never quit" or "always stay the course." Staying the course only makes sense if you're headed in the right direction, and my mother has no idea where you're headed or if your dreams align with your talents. Thus you will not find much here in the way of advice. What you will find is *encouragement*. The same kind of encouragement she offered me, as I struggled for years to produce a TV show that people would watch. The same kind of encouragement my dad offered to her, with every unsolicited public reading of her latest work.

When I asked my mother what she wanted her readers to take from this book, she said, "I want people—especially aspiring writers—to see me as a cheerleader, standing on the sidelines of a marathon, offering them cups of cool water as they stumble toward the finish line."

Which is, of course, precisely how I have always felt in her company.

As always, I sent my mom a draft of this—my worst foreword to date—and as always, she corrected my spelling errors and called me to say thanks.

"See?" she said. "That wasn't so hard, was it?"

"Piece of cake," I said. "I wrote the whole thing in half an hour."

"I can tell," she said. "And I love the way you put so much of yourself into it! The way you mentioned all those different TV shows you work on. So clever!"

"Well, you know what they say, Mom—celebrity sells!"

"Oh, good," she said. "Because my fourth book is nearly finished, and I was wondering...."

Chapter 1

GETTING IT WRITE

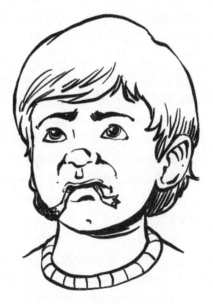

I T WAS 2018, AND I WAS WAITING NERVOUSLY ON THE sidelines as the manager of a Barnes & Noble bookstore stood at the microphone in front of a packed audience. He was holding up my first published book—and smiling.

Nearby, an elderly gentleman stood in an aisle between the bookshelves, holding up a camera. He looked for all the world like a proud parent at a graduation ceremony.

"I bought this *New York Times* best-seller *About My Mother* as a Christmas gift," the manager said. "But first, I sat down to read a few pages. Two days later, I had read it from cover to cover and loved every word! Then I wrapped it and presented it to my mother, who also read it from cover to cover—and *she* laughed out loud on every page. It's my pleasure to introduce first-time author Peggy Rowe. *An overnight success—at the age of eighty!*"

My mind was still focused on his introduction as I thanked him and the enthusiastic audience. Then I smiled in the direction of the elderly gentleman—my husband, John. *Overnight success indeed!* I thought. As though I had sat down at the computer one day in my late seventies and decided to give this writing thing a try. The humorist in me wanted to laugh out loud. If they only knew...

Long before I was a published author, I was on a journey—a writing journey that took me along a winding road filled with potholes and detours, a hairpin turn or two, and some pretty magnificent scenery. It was a road that would have come to a dead-end twenty years earlier had fate not stepped in.

This wasn't the first interesting introduction that got my attention. Some years earlier, in the mid-1990s, my husband and I were at a social gathering when John ran into an old teaching colleague. After they exchanged greetings, he introduced me. "I don't believe you've met my wife. This is Peggy; she's a writer."

It was the first time I'd heard myself described in that way, and I would have corrected John right then and there. But he said it in much the same manner a parent might mention that Johnny had just made the dean's list, and I didn't have the heart. I waited and made my feelings known in the car on the way home.

"John, you cannot tell people I'm a writer when I haven't even been published. It makes me feel like a phony."

"I beg your pardon! You *are* a writer! You go to writers' conferences, you belong to critique groups, you take writing courses...."

"You took a photography course; it didn't make you a photographer. And what am I supposed to say when people ask me what I've written? 'Oh, I write humorous poetry for special occasions. And if you need a creative eulogy for a funeral, I'm your girl.' *That* does not make me a writer."

"Hon, you've written a book; you're finishing another one. You write all the time! In fact, you should enroll in Writers Anonymous. I wake up in the middle of the night...you're at the computer. I look up from the Lord's Prayer in church...you're making notes on the back of the morning bulletin! We're in the middle of dinner...you're making a beeline to the desk. And you're not fooling me one bit when you roll over in bed and turn on your light. I only hope you're answering a *creative* urge and not rating my performance."

"No," I smiled. "For that, I hold up a finger or two." My husband looked over at me and frowned. "Or nine or ten," I added.

"Anyway, that's what makes you a writer!" John laughed. "Well, that and a dusty house, a pile of ironing that's taller than I am, and the crop of mold in the vegetable drawer of the fridge."

"And you can't refer to a manuscript that's collecting dust on the bottom shelf as a book! I have a folder full of rejection slips that prove it's no good."

"They prove nothing! Look how far you've come. Everybody loves your writing, Maggie! I've even seen your writing make people laugh at a funeral."

Loved ones cannot be objective. It's one of the things I've learned at writers' conferences over the years. And it's why my husband has always been a lousy critic. He claims to like everything I write. Whenever I complete a story—no matter what it is—John reads it aloud to me, so that I can hear it and make it better. It was, and continues to be, a valuable aid for revision. Often he reads the same passages multiple times—without complaint—claiming to love it every time.

Though he *was* right about my poems. More than once they had revived a party where the guests looked as if they had inhaled chloroform. And it was true that I had brought laughter to mourners at my friend's funeral service....

<< ◆ >>

I couldn't believe Ann was making such an unreasonable request—and from her deathbed, no less—when she knew I couldn't refuse.

"Oh, Peggy," she whispered, "I've put my family through hell these past three years. Would you please speak at my funeral and make them laugh? Or smile?"

I lay awake that night. How in the world do you make a grieving family laugh when they're burying their beloved wife and mother?

I reminded myself that it was humor, after all, that had defined our relationship. Two wives and mothers bonding over the travails of family life and laughing at our cellulite, spider veins, and vanishing waistlines. Of course, much of our "girl talk" had been personal, but I had years of material to draw on.

I could do this. I sat down at my computer and wrote my very best humor.

At the service, I stood between Ann's open casket and her family seated at the front of an overflowing room. An exhausted and tearful husband, children (who had grown up with my own sons), grandchildren, brothers, nieces, nephews, cousins . . . all waiting—tissues in hand—for me to extoll the admirable qualities of this remarkable woman.

And so I began, hoping for some sympathetic smiles. Without notes and meeting their gaze, I spoke of my friend's dying request and asked for their support. There were looks of skepticism. I wasn't surprised.

"When I left my administrative job in our church's preschool, Ann assumed my position," I explained. "I was all too familiar with the challenges of the job—the committee oversight, the preacher's intrusive daily check-ins, parental expectations, and unreasonable health department demands. Not to mention the daily supervision of thirteen classroom teachers and aides and the one hundred precious 'angels' in our care. Oh yeah, there was stress galore, and I knew from experience that sharing stories would be therapeutic—essential, even—to my friend's sanity."

"Peggy, you won't believe this," Ann had said on one of her calls. "Ms. Clark came in today to register her three-year-old. After our interview, I asked her, 'Does Donny have any unusual words for using the bathroom that his teachers should know about?' Without hesitation, she responded, 'No, nothing unusual. But sometimes when he goes stinky, he forgets to push Mr. Beeper down and winkles on the wall.' But no unusual words."

There was actual laughter! And I silently thanked God.

I told them about another call from Ann after she had gone into the three- and four-year-olds room and discovered a child taped to his chair with yards of masking tape. Another child had a strip of masking tape across his mouth.

"As teachers, we laughed together because we were well aware of the temptations. But as administrators and mothers, we were horrified and arranged for an immediate staff refresher course in classroom management and disciplinary strategies."

"I told Ann about my unforgettable first day on that same job and the *warm* welcome I had received from two-year-old Stacey, who looked me square in the eye, gritted her little teeth, and screamed, 'I hate you, poopie face!' And there was wide-eyed four-year-old Eric, who had looked at his teacher in wonder and innocence and exclaimed, 'Miss Jean, you have *big* boobies!'"

Then, over exceptionally loud laughter, I said, "Miss Jean is here today, if you'd like to introduce yourself." (I had considered saying, "You'll recognize her," but that seemed a bit too *on the nose*, as it were. I was glad I had spoken to her beforehand.)

I like to think that my friend, reclining on a pillow of satin nearby, was comforted by my final gift that afternoon, as chuckles and laughter filled the air. I couldn't remember a time when I had found laughter more comforting.

In the end, Ann's "unreasonable request" was a piece of cake. Especially when compared to the memorial service of an old college friend. When Bill's family asked me to say a few words, I considered refusing.

What does one say about a man who had been unfaithful and verbally abusive to his wife—my close friend of many years? I made the tough decision and agreed—then faced the writing challenge of a lifetime.

Instead of addressing Bill the husband, and his shortcomings—he did, after all, have children who loved him—I spoke of Bill the friend, who had visited me in the hospital through the years to show his concern; who had shown up at our door with a pot of soup when John and I were both ill; and who had helped us to mourn at my parents' funerals—shedding genuine tears of compassion. The only humor of the day came after my talk, when mutual friends quietly complimented me on my *editing* skills.

≪ ◆ ≫

Thinking back, my husband had a point about me being a writer. It had become my life. And it was almost a curse. When I wasn't at my computer, I was reading books on the subject or thinking about a story. I woke up in the middle of the night to jot down an idea or to finish an entire chapter. I wrote when my arthritis was aching. I wrote while waiting for a colonoscopy. Oh yeah, I wrote when I should have been dusting or cleaning out the refrigerator. And no, I've never written during moments of passion—please, give me some credit!—though I can't guarantee you that my mind wasn't outlining a story.

If I'd had credentials in journalism, I could have been a decent reporter. I interviewed everyone I met, from the used car salesman who told me about a test-drive that ended in a carjacking at gunpoint, to an undertaker who spoke of a "client" who had chosen to be buried in her valuable full-length mink coat so that her greedy daughter-in-law wouldn't get it.

The truth was, I had come a long way from that timid woman who would rather clean a crusty oven than share her writing. Just as a butterfly emerges from a cocoon and discovers the wonders of nature, I had emerged from the shadows and discovered the true reward of creative writing— which is, of course, sharing.

One presenter at a writers' conference actually told the class, "Sharing your work isn't important. The important thing in writing is to feel fulfilled."

As my husband would say, "Hogwash!"

For sure, personal fulfillment is important, but writing is a two-way street—a conversation. What is the point of a story or a poem if it is never heard or read? If it doesn't move, entertain, or inspire someone? If it doesn't enlighten or comfort someone? And on occasion, even horrify or disgust someone?

It was the early 1960s when I discovered the joy of writing and sharing. I was fresh out of college and teaching third grade in the Baltimore County public schools. It was long before I thought of myself as a writer and decades before being published.

My class was about to begin a unit on animals, and I had decided to introduce it with a poem. What better way to spark the children's interest and imagination? So I began searching through poetry books. Meanwhile, my husband and I were taking a walk through the woods behind our apartment when we came upon a box turtle and *voilà*, I had my introduction.

The problem was, I needed a poem more visual than the ones I'd found in books, so I sat down and wrote my own. I called it "Turtles." With a live box turtle moseying across the floor at the front of the classroom, I read my original poem aloud—to rave reviews.

What was meant as motivation for the students had a surprising result. The children's enthusiasm for my poetry was the motivation I needed for further writing and sharing. My "epiphany" happened on the school playground at recess the day I came upon a group of my girls chanting *my* poems from memory, while jumping rope to the rhythmic, rhyming meter. It was better even than seeing a bonus in my paycheck! (Although my husband might not see it that way.) One of their favorites was "Turtles."

Turtles

Turtles are poky
Wherever they go.
They carry their houses,
That's why they're so slow.

When playing on grass,
Or crossing the street,
They're dragging their shelter
On four tiny feet.

And when they get tired,
Wherever they roam,
They're lucky to have
Their own mobile home.

If raindrops should fall
When they've gone to town,
They don't have to wonder
If windows are down.

When leaving for school,
Or shopping at stores,
They don't have to bother
To lock their front doors.

Sure, turtles are slow,
But you would be too.
If you had to carry
Your whole house with you!

It didn't take me long to realize that little boys pay close attention to—and willingly memorize—irreverent, nonsensical, and even rude poetry. So I happily accommodated them with a reading/language activity to their liking. Perhaps a science unit on health.

Nutrition

My neighbor Tom eats bugs and worms,
And bark from apple trees.
You'd think he'd get a stomachache,
Or catch some bad disease.

One day he chased a little frog,
That hopped into our yard.
He caught it, stuffed it in his mouth,
Blinked twice and swallowed hard.

My sister said she saw him eat
A tiny, shiny rock.
One morning he took off his shoe,
And ate his smelly sock.

Last summer on July the fourth,
He ate a cherry bomb…
Then took off like a rocket ship,
And now we can't find Tom.

I'm not sure I could get away with using my original homespun poetry in today's structured, transparent classroom environment—no matter how enriching. Though I'm confident they inflicted no harm on my captive audience—and taught me the true joy of sharing. The ultimate reward comes when the writing we share makes a difference in someone's life. When this someone is your seven-year-old son, it's all the sweeter.

<< ◆ >>

It was in the early 1970s the afternoon Scott came home in tears, threw his books on the sofa, and declared, "I'm never going back to that school! My teacher yells like a banshee all day long, and she spits when she's screaming! I can't stand it!"

I was aware of his teacher's reputation; indeed, the entire school knew that she was at the end of her teaching career, as well as at the end of her rope, and she was struggling to hold on until the end. She reminded me of an old herding dog who, after a long, devoted career, turns on the sheep he is meant to guide and protect—and is forced into retirement.

After that day, I did two things: I began volunteering in the classroom once a week and encouraged other mothers to do the same. It somewhat lowered the decibel level in the room from that of, say, a running motorcycle engine to that of normal conversation.

My most rewarding solution was a humorous poem I wrote to share with the sweetest, smartest seven-year-old ever. "While she's screaming on the outside, Scott," I told him, "you just think about this poem and laugh on the inside!" It was our little secret, this short poem...until now.

The Banshee

When I was in the second grade,
My teacher loved to scream.
Just inches from my face she'd shout.
Her volume was extreme.

She shrieked and yelled from nine to three,
Her voice was terrifying,
Her eyes bugged out, her lips curled back,
And then the spit came flying.

I feared that I would drown that year,
Saliva filled the air.
I kept a towel inside my desk,
To dry my face and hair.

She really didn't have a clue,
That screaming, spitting teacher.
A student's never going to learn,
From such a fearsome creature!

≪ ◆ ≫

I decided John was right. If working in a garden every day growing vegetables or flowers makes one a gardener, and if reading a book every week makes one a reader, and if running a few miles a day makes one a runner, then I was a writer—published or not.

I had certainly done my homework. I looked forward to Tuesday evenings and hanging out with fellow writers the way a school kid looks forward to Friday afternoons and playing with friends. A professor from a recent creative writing course at the community college had invited four students to join him in a critique group. For a couple of hours a week, we sat around a table at the local Barnes & Noble café drinking coffee and reading our work aloud. Not only did I experience the power of positive critique and benefit from the group's ideas, I grew comfortable with criticism—and learned when to ignore it and follow my own instincts.

My most valuable critique ever was the result of ignoring the advice I had heard in writing courses and at writers' seminars through the years: "Don't ask family members to read your writing! They love you, so of course they want to love your work. You will not get an honest assessment." And didn't I know it!

That didn't stop me from sharing my first book, a middle-grade novel, with my young granddaughters.

Three-year-old Jessica listened while building with LEGOs, putting a puzzle together, or coloring a picture. Then there was Katie, who had been an early reader. I remember the Christmas she was four and read a children's picture book aloud to my sister, Janet, a career first-grade teacher.

"She's memorized it, of course," said Janet.

"No, she really reads," I said. So my sister turned to the glossary in the back of the book and asked Katie to read the list of vocabulary words—which she did, perfectly. Now seven, Katie sat beside me, captivated, as we took turns reading about a nerdy young boy who wanted nothing more than to be left alone with his books.

I religiously avoid lofty phrases such as, *My heart soared,* or *The angels sang,* or *The sound of a heavenly choir descended from the clouds.* That said, when it was time for dinner or bed and my granddaughter pleaded, "Oh Grandmom, just one more chapter—please!"...well, I'll just say that such reactions brought overwhelming joy to this grandmother and writer. So much so, in fact, that I began sharing other age-appropriate writings with my homegrown, mini-focus group.

One evening, as Jessica lay asleep in the next bed, I sat beside Katie and read aloud my latest short story. When I finished, my granddaughter gave me a concise critique:

"I like the story, Grandmom," she said, "but you need to put the good parts closer together."

A seven-year-old had just told me that I needed to lose the parts that people skip and keep only the good parts. It was great advice that I've applied to everything I have written to this day!

Who knew that putting words on paper could be so rewarding?

And who knew that putting words on paper could bring such heartache?

Chapter 2

PLAYING THE GAME

MY HUSBAND DOESN'T CALL ME POLLYANNA FOR nothing, as I'm famous for seeing the positive side of things. Ask anybody who knows me. It's a trait that came in handy while raising children and teaching. There was that afternoon many years ago, for instance, when Mike and Scott brought their eighteen-month-old brother, Phil, to the back door to show off their "artwork."

"Look what we did, Mommy!" Mike said proudly.

"It's our creation—from the wild cherry tree!" Scott added, giggling.

My precious toddler was covered in creepy crawly caterpillars—his nose, ears, hair, arms, legs ....

I could easily have screamed (very loudly), but as Phil was giggling, too, I could see the humor and simply reminded them, "Caterpillars go poopie, you know!"

"That's okay," one of them said. "We'll wash him off in the stream." (And no! That did not happen!)

Then there was that day some years later when ten-year-old Skippy looked me in the eye and said, "I don't have to listen you! You're not my teacher; you're just a substitute!"

Instead of getting angry, I was able to smile sweetly and say, "You know what? You're right, Skippy. You don't have to listen to me. You go on down to the office now and listen to Mr. Royston for a while."

But even Pollyanna had her limits ....

With two unpublished manuscripts collecting dust on the shelf and enough rejection slips to paper the walls of our church sanctuary, Pollyanna had left the building.

In college, I'd worked hard and followed the rules— by attending classes on time all the time, completing assignments, and studying for tests. And my hard work had been rewarded with a degree and a teaching career. I had "played the game" equally as hard at my writing craft and hoped for similar results from the publishing world.

In the early 1980s, years before email submissions, I wrote exemplary query letters, tons of them, all adhering to the publishers' strict rule: No simultaneous submissions! Which meant sending to only one publisher at a time, though I knew plenty of writers who didn't comply. I followed formatting guidelines faithfully: wide margins, double-spaced lines, twelve-point black type on the whitest of paper, sent off in a neatly addressed manila envelope including an SASE (self-addressed stamped envelope). My submissions had everything but a blessing from the Pope.

I knew what it was to walk to the mailbox day after day for months—with hope in my heart and a prayer on my lips—until that dreaded rejection notice appeared, only to repeat the process with another publisher, and another, and another. And doing my crying in private. The defeat was that personal. Nowadays, with the advent of electronic submissions, the process is way more civilized. A writer can send off a query or article or story in an email before breakfast and be in tears before lunch. Ah, progress.

So after years of disappointment, *I showed them*! I quit the discouraging process and stepped away from writing altogether. It was time to move on. Opening one more envelope with a rejection slip bordered on masochism.

For two years, with my book manuscripts languishing out of sight in a drawer, I stayed away from writing, turning my attention to gardening with houseplants on every windowsill, flower beds, and a vegetable garden that attracted rabbits and deer from neighboring zip codes. I took a knitting course at the local high school and made caps and mittens and Christmas stockings. I took a quilting class and immersed myself in cutting, piecing, and sewing fabric. I made a quilt for our bed, one for each of our three sons, and for the dog's bed—all the while mentally composing articles for horticulture publications as well as quilting and stitching magazines.

And then fate stepped in. How well I remember that day in 1997 when a letter appeared in my mailbox I would have happily traded for a dozen rejection notices—the results from my annual mammogram. I was fifty-nine, and *rejection* was suddenly no longer the most dreaded word in my vocabulary. It had been replaced by an entire dictionary of terrifying terms: needle biopsy, ductile carcinoma, surgery, radiation, depression, and cancer support group. Writing two children's books was but a fond, yet disappointing memory with the writing community a thing of the past.

The surrounding darkness was reminiscent of an abandoned coal mine we had visited when the kids were young. There was complete lack of light—palpable, isolating, debilitating. The humor had evaporated from my world, and there was nothing to look forward to.

One evening son Mike visited, and I tried to explain what it felt like to be me. "I have *no* control over my life," I told him.

"Mom," he said, "if you have ever had material dropped in your lap, it's now. You're a writer. Sit down and write about *this* chapter of your life. How do you feel when you wake up in the morning? How has it affected Dad? And your relationship? And while you're at it, find some humor! You can do it!"

"Look at me, Michael Rowe!" I screamed. "Do I look like somebody who's going to sit down and write a funny story? I can't even think, much less write!"

But he was having none of it.

"Think about the people you love. Do it for Dad. Do it for Scott and Phil and me—and your granddaughters.

Write it for the thousands of women out there who have had a similar diagnosis—people you'll never meet."

"You don't get it, Mike. I can write it. And I can make it good. But I can't get it published, and I can't take the rejection. But you wouldn't know about that. It saps your self-confidence, your self-worth…."

And then he had the nerve to laugh right in front of his mother who had cancer.

"Mom, I'm a performer. I'm in show business. I've done freelance work. *Rejection* is my middle name. I haven't told you about all the auditions I've had that ended in rejection. Just write your story for now. And maybe someday you can share it. And make a difference."

So I did. And I was grateful that my son had the grace not to tell me to stop thinking about myself.

I survived the treatment and spent two years in a cancer support group making new friends and losing them, feeling angry, feeling fortunate, feeling guilty—and journaling *every step of the way* with humor and optimism when possible. At the end, I wrote my story, and years later during Breast Cancer Awareness Month (October), Mike published it on his social media page. It was read by millions who left thousands of poignant and heartwarming comments.

"Finding the Humor and Making a Difference"
(The people in my story were real, though I changed their names. The Wellness Community is now HopeWell Cancer Support in Baltimore.)

Certain events in our lives are unforgettable: the birth of a child, the death of a parent, an anxiously awaited telephone call from the doctor. Even now, decades later, I still remember every word.

My husband handed me the phone as I sat up in bed.

"I have the pathology from your surgery, Mrs. Rowe," said the doctor. I tilted the phone so John could hear.

"It's good news," he said. John and I exhaled and exchanged grateful glances as I ran my fingers over the white bandage protruding from the top of my nightgown.

"It was a ductile carcinoma, and we got good margins. My secretary will give you an appointment to remove the stitches next week. We'll have a chat then; bring your hubby along."

After making another appointment, we said goodbye, and John returned the phone to the kitchen with a spring in his step I hadn't seen in weeks.

"Hey, hon, get that medical dictionary from the book-case," I called out to him, reaching for my robe and real-izing that for the first time in days, I felt hungry.

John leafed through the pages.

"Ductal carcinoma . . . ductal carcinoma . . . ductal . . . ."

As he read, I listened, stunned. At the age of fifty-nine, I did, indeed, have breast cancer. We looked at each other wondering what the *good* news was.

The following week our question was answered. The good news was that I'd had my regular mammogram— the picture that exposed a small tumor before it could breach the walls of the milk duct and spread.

"We caught it in the early stages," the doctor said.

Days later, an oncologist explained that errant cancer cells might have broken away from the tumor.

"It just takes one small cell," he warned—and prescribed thirty rounds of radiation "just in case."

No big deal we told ourselves. It was less traumatic than chemotherapy. During that first session, lying flat with my arm resting over my head, a purple grid was tattooed onto the target area. The following week after the incision had healed, I pulled on a wrinkled blue gown and lay on a table in the cavernous treatment room while technicians manipulated a monster machine. When it was positioned just above the grid, they told me to lie perfectly still, then scurried away, taking refuge behind a bunker at the back of the room.

A red light flashed, a loud buzzer sounded, and the linear accelerator droned. I tried not to think of the doctor's warning of possible damage to my heart, lung, and other healthy tissue. It was over in no time—for that day. The next day, same drill: flashing light, deafening beeping buzzer, scurrying techs. It was the London Blitz, and I was left alone on the streets with the lethal rays while technicians disappeared down into the bomb shelters.

Two months was an eternity not to shower or use soap. Clothing felt like medieval chain mail over the painful, persistent, seeping red rash. I checked off the treatments on a calendar. On day fifteen, swallowing became difficult, and I decided to discontinue the radiation. The oncologist strongly warned that doing so would render the current treatment ineffective.

Once famous for humming cheerfully around the house and a perpetual smile, I began crying for no apparent reason. The smallest challenge tried my patience, and my husband found himself living with a stranger who flew into a rage at the least provocation. Through tears, I spoke with a nurse practitioner at the radiation center.

"You're suffering from depression," she said, and mentioned the name of a cancer support group.

"I don't need a support group!" I told her. "I have family and supportive friends."

"You say you're always close to tears, you're angry, and your behavior's irrational. That sounds like depression." It was true and uncharacteristic of me.

"Here you go," she said, handing me a brochure. "The Wellness Community is an amazing place. Believe me, nobody understands you like other people who are going through the same thing. Give it a try!"

I put the paper in my purse and forgot about it—until the following morning when my husband made a ridiculous, unreasonable suggestion.

"You should get out of the house and take a walk on such a beautiful day, hon."

So naturally, I did the only logical thing. I picked up a saltshaker and hurled it at his head. Thanks to quick reflexes, John ducked in time. While he was hiding the kitchen knives, I made an appointment.

On Tuesday afternoon I found myself at the Wellness Community sitting with a group of seven strangers—adult men and women, young and old, from opposite ends of the economic spectrum, all struggling to cope with the stress of living with cancer. I had no way of knowing then just how dramatic my introduction to the group would be.

Our leader—a compassionate, experienced psychotherapist—kept the conversation flowing, as well as boxes of tissues and chocolates. I hadn't yet spoken when I helped myself to a piece of Whitman's candy, then stood up and carried the box to Bill, who was lying on a sofa with a pillow beneath his head. Still recovering from his latest round of chemo, the middle-aged man had been met at curbside with a wheelchair that day. I was holding out the box of candy when I suddenly tripped over Bill's shoes. As chocolates fell onto his face and neck, I fell awkwardly onto his body with my hand in an unfortunate place. Appalled, I shot to my feet fearful that I had inflicted mortal damage on this poor, suffering soul.

"Oh, I'm so sorry," I said.

Bill casually rolled a soft-center chocolate from his chin, into his mouth, chuckled, and said something along the lines of, "Believe me, it was my pleasure. This is the first time I've smiled in days."

The group laughed along with Bill and me, and when it was my turn to speak, I shared my cancer story. I finished with the saltshaker incident, hoping I wouldn't be judged too harshly.

"Oh, that's nothing," Carol said. "I threw a plate of sausages at my husband the other morning—for no reason at all."

When I recalled tears of frustration over a painful radiation rash and trouble swallowing, Betty told us about breaking down in the grocery store when she couldn't find her favorite cereal.

Annie told us about trying to open the driveway gate that very morning. "I pushed, and when it wouldn't budge, I laid my head on my arm and sobbed—until my husband came to my rescue. So out of character for me ...." she said, shaking her head.

Later in the session when the leader brought in a bowl of seedless green grapes and headed for Bill, he held up his hand and said emphatically, "I want Peggy to deliver mine."

Over the following months, I was buoyed by members' courageous optimism and saddened by their despair. Nobody gave advice or told someone else how they should feel.

I felt like a fraud, sharing my limelight with people in the latter stages of the disease and suffering from the devastating effects of chemo. When I heard there was a waiting list for Tuesday afternoons, I offered to drop out and make space for someone more deserving. But our leader convinced me that my presence was important to the group dynamic.

"Please stay, Peggy!" she urged. "Each person brings something special. Your sense of humor is a breath of fresh air."

And so I continued on, long after my treatment ended and our kitchen knives were returned to the drawer. Long after my burning radiation rash faded, and I could resume showering. Long after I could swallow normally, I supported my Tuesday "family."

I was embarrassed the day Nadine shared an intimate story with us. "Since my chemo and hormone treatments, something really strange has happened!" she said. "Whenever I sneeze, I have an orgasm."

I wasn't sure if she was serious, but we all laughed, and I asked her if she had reported this to her health care provider. "Maybe they can do something for you," I suggested, with an innocent expression.

"Oh, I will," she said. "When I get around to it." There was more laughter.

The following week as we were celebrating her birthday with cake and ice cream, I handed Nadine a small gift. "It isn't much, but I hope it brings you pleasure," I said, as she unwrapped the small can of black pepper and laughed until ginger ale bubbled from her nose.

"Do *not* open that here!" I warned her, shaking my finger. Once again, laughter erupted from the group.

We cheered when someone's blood count improved, when an MRI confirmed no new tumor growth, and when Judy donned a new wig. The Tuesday afternoon when thirty-five-year-old Sandra sashayed through the door with her newly grown hair *and* sporting an outstanding pair of newly reconstructed breasts, we oohed and aahed and celebrated with two round cakes, each with a Hershey's Kiss in the center.

There were unspoken prayers for Carol as she traveled to far-off hospitals for experimental treatments—and mourning when those treatments failed. I shed genuine tears of grief at Bill's funeral and was outraged when Doris's husband announced that he could no longer cope with her cancer—and left her, alone.

A year and a half after joining the support group, I shared with them how cancer had changed my life. I talked about the harmless cough and stiff neck that sent me racing to the doctor. And I told them about an embarrassing trip to a specialist.

"I woke up one morning and noticed a swelling on either side of my nose," I said. "I was convinced that my cancer had returned. My doctor referred me to an ENT, the same one who had removed our children's tonsils.

"During the examination, he peered at me over his glasses, and in a fatherly, Dr. Marcus Welby impersonation, said, 'I'm going to be honest with you, Mrs. Rowe.' I braced myself—some rare type of rhino-cancer, undoubtedly—leaving me horribly disfigured before I would finally lose my struggle. Then he put his hand on my arm and with a twinkle in his eye, said, 'In all my years of practice, I have never seen, nor have I heard of, a case of breast cancer metastasizing to the nose.'" The group laughed along with me.

On my final visit to the Wellness Community, a full two years after joining, I shared the story of the rare "cancer" on my hand. The suspicious white streak on my knuckle had appeared one evening after my shower and by the following morning, was surrounded by redness and swelling. My GP referred me to a surgeon. In a sterile theater, wearing a mask and gown, he removed a foreign body from my hand that was roughly one-half inch in length and looked to be wooden.

My husband brought it home in a jar, examined it under a magnifying glass, took a picture of it beside a toothpick, and pronounced it, "the most expensive splinter in the history of medicine." When company comes, John shows it off like it's the Hope Diamond. "Yes sirree," he says, "the golden spike!"

≪ ◆ ≫

At the end of my cancer ordeal, I put my story aside and returned to my small writing group. I had missed my two buddies, Donna and Elizabeth, both fine writers—unfailingly supportive. Still, writing was an uphill climb. After cancer, everything else seemed frivolous.

One weekend Elizabeth and Donna drove to an out-of-town writers' conference. On their return, Elizabeth handed me a magazine.

"Peg, the editor of this horse publication is looking for stories! You speak *horse,* and you're so good with short stories. Why don't you put your novels aside for now and concentrate on shorter pieces—to submit."

"I agree," said Donna. "That story you wrote about your scary childhood dentist is hilarious! People will love your humor. Give it a try, Peg! What do you have to lose?"

They were right, of course. I had survived my cancer ordeal, just as my seven-year-old son had survived his banshee decades earlier. The risk of rejection paled in comparison.

So I climbed back on my horse and began writing every day—short stories and essays. Lots of them— without knowing if they would ever be read. While I was at it, I composed a nonsense poem for a contest at an upcoming book fair I'd seen advertised. But I still wasn't ready to submit my work to publishers. Not yet. In truth, I was merely satisfying my addiction to storytelling. What fun it was moving the small bits and fragments of stories around like puzzle pieces, looking for the best fit and experiencing the satisfaction of an interesting tale.

I came across the story about my scary childhood dentist that Donna had referred to. It was one of the first short stories I had written and was as much about my mother as it was my dentist. She was the mother who was always in charge. The mother who had reacted to my cancer diagnosis in a predictable manner.

"Peggy," she said, "You do not have cancer! You just have some calcification, that's all. You're going to be fine."

I knew she needed to believe that. I also knew she cried as she walked across the lawn back to her house.

Donna was right. The dentist story had enough humor for a Carol Burnett skit—even if it was a tad on the dark side....

"A Winning Smile"

If my mother said it once, she said it a hundred times: "Peggy, your best friend is your toothbrush. If you take care of your teeth, your teeth will take care of you!" Then she'd flash me that winning smile, showing a row of perfect, white teeth—without one filling. I was treated to a similar pitch at the dinner table when faced with a dish of hot, steamy turnip greens, kale, spinach, or collard greens. They were always served with a side of sage wisdom: "Teeth and gums love leafy green vegetables, Peggy; I grew up on them."

I'm here to tell you that not even a puddle of melted butter on top could make those disgusting greens tasty to a kid, but it wasn't as though I had a choice. Not that I ever actually chewed them. Thank God for cows and the milk that could wash the offensive food straight down the gullet without chewing. And forget dessert, unless we had company, or it was a special occasion like somebody's birthday. Because as everybody knows, sugar causes cavities.

My mother must have known what she was talking about because trips to the dentist were rare—except for the occasional childhood checkup where she stood beside the chair beaming as Dr. Neiman praised my dental hygiene and pronounced me cavity-free. Mom would put her head back and sniff—taking all the credit. Once, on the drive home, we passed the Paramount Theatre where the name Errol Flynn was on the marquee. I heard her say as if to herself, "Hmm . . . Dr. Neiman reminds me of Errol Flynn."

And then I turned that magic age of nine and was deemed old enough to go to the dentist by myself. Instead of accompanying me and standing beside the chair during my checkups, my mother took to dropping me off at the front steps like I was the daily newspaper. Then she'd drive to the shops a block away, and I'd meet her afterwards at the Acme or Woolworth's— of course, after a lecture about crossing Belair Road at the traffic light.

That's when my trips to the dentist took a decidedly dark turn. Instead of engaging in cheerful conversation with Mom, Dr. Neiman and his assistant, Marilyn, joked with each other like I wasn't even sitting there between them. Next thing I knew, Errol Flynn was announcing that I had a couple of cavities and would need to be numbed so that I wouldn't feel the drill. He said it in the same casual tone as saying, "It's a beautiful day," as though it were a rite of passage and no big deal.

I must have looked alarmed because his friendly assistant patted me on the shoulder and said, "It'll be over in a second, and then we just wait a few minutes while it gets numb."

"I'll do one today, and you can come back next week for the second one," the dentist said.

"Hold your horses!" I wanted to say. "No way! Uh-uh, you've made a mistake! I don't get cavities! I brush my teeth! I eat kale and turnip greens and spinach...."

I didn't know which was worse: the pain of the needle, the sound of the drill, the numbness of my tongue and lip, or knowing I'd have to tell my mother that I had *two cavities*. I was left alone while the novocain performed its magic, but I always knew where Dr. Neiman and Marilyn were, as I could hear them chuckling and whispering somewhere behind my chair. When it was over, Marilyn reminded me not to bite my numb lips, and I left.

My mother's reaction to the news was disappointment and dismay—initially. Then she squinted her eyes and wondered ... "Peggy, are you sure you're brushing? Top and bottom, inside and out?" Then she accused me of sneaking candy. The following week as the dentist drilled and filled the second cavity, there was more of the same. Numbing...giggling...whispering...

Six months later, there was another cavity, with two more needles and longer to wait for numbing—with moaning behind the chair. I was just an innocent kid, but I wasn't stupid. I confided in my mother after witnessing some affectionate behavior between "Errol Flynn" and "Miss Congeniality."

"Oh, you're mistaken," she said. "He's in the Lions Club with Dad! He's a husband and father, for goodness sake. His wife is right upstairs in their apartment. *Do not spread ugly rumors like that, Peggy!*"

With more approaching appointments, there were nightmares. The trepidation began in earnest when I entered the tall, two-story house—my heart pounding like the hoofbeats of a Thoroughbred coming down the stretch at Timonium Race Track. Every detail of those visits is etched in my memory: the way Daddy's name was etched in his bowling trophies, the stark waiting room with a faint odor of disinfectant, the row of wooden chairs reminiscent of the Greyhound Bus terminal where we picked up visiting relatives, and the table with neatly arranged magazines. As though a person could enjoy reading, knowing what loomed on the other side of the office door.

It was the enormous oak grandfather clock in the corner that dominated the waiting room—the long pendulum swinging back and forth, back and forth, ticking off the minutes and bringing me closer to that "Armageddon" our preacher talked about. It was like that clock on the wall in the movie *High Noon*—bringing Gary Cooper closer to the treacherous outlaws committed to finishing him off.

The office door would eventually open, like I knew it would, and some poor bloodied and numbed soul would hurry to freedom. A minute later, Marilyn would appear with her full, red lips, thick glasses, and large facial pores.

"Are we ready for the doctor?" she would ask, all bubbly, like it was my turn on a carnival ride—the carnival ride from hell. I wanted to scream and run for the hills. But I'd only have to face my mother, who could be as scary as any dentist.

It was the 1940s, long before child-friendly dentistry with colorful uniforms, patient bibs with frolicking puppy dogs, happy music in the background, and spinning mobiles hanging from the ceiling to take your mind off the gruesome business at hand. It was also a time before fluoride in the water, high-speed drills, X-rays, and second opinions.

An appointment could go on for hours because when it came to my treatment, Dr. Neiman had carte blanche. He could cut the nose right off my face and my mother would say, "Well, you're the doctor, Mr. Flynn—uh, I mean, Dr. Neiman." There was always a cavity requiring novocain and multiple jabs. I had a nickname for him, which my parents said was disrespectful.

"Maybe if you come with me like you used to, *Dr. Needleman* won't find a cavity," I told Mom. But she had already reconciled my plight with the fact that I had soft teeth like my father. Needleman had pulled all of Dad's teeth two years earlier.

I was ten years old that day I saw my dentist reach out and grab his assistant's rear end the way you might pluck a ripe peach from a low-hanging branch. Surely, I was imagining things. I had, after all, just been jabbed with three needles filled with enough novocain to stop a bull elephant dead in his tracks, and my eyes were teary. All I knew was, one minute Dr. Neiman was on my right removing the needle from my mouth, and Marilyn was on my left, filling a small paper cup with water, and the next, my dentist's hand was grabbing his assistant's bottom and pulling her backwards across the floor—like he was reeling in the catch of the day.

I didn't dare look, but I can tell you there was a lot of commotion behind me—squealing and giggling—like when my teenage sister and her girlfriends had sleepovers. I sat frozen, as though the novocain had gone straight to my brain, rendering me deaf, dumb, and blind. I wondered if Mrs. Needleman ever dropped into the office ... unannounced.

Like most ten-year-olds back in the 1940s, I wasn't good at grasping lust and lechery. Besides, these two medical professionals looked every bit as pure as the driven snow—he in a spotless white coat and she in a starched white uniform and polished shoes. It pained my eyes to look directly at them when the bright light was on. It was a lot to process. Dr. Neiman was a Lion, for Pete's sake. One thing I was sure of: Daddy would never treat Mom in such a way—yet this woman was all giggly and didn't seem to mind at all. Like I said, it was a lot for an immature ten-year-old to process.

Suddenly, a pointed nose, round glasses, pencil-thin mustache, and dark slicked-back hair appeared just inches from my numbing face. Here's the weird part. He was panting, like my old dog after chasing a rabbit on a summer day. Except that Needleman's tongue wasn't hanging out. Or at least, I don't think it was. It's hard to remember. Perhaps he was having a major coronary event like my parent's old friend, Glenn, who had played baseball in 90-degree weather at a church picnic and been carted off in an ambulance. I didn't know what Errol Flynn looked like, but as far as I was concerned, my dentist was a dead ringer for the villain who tied the girl to the railroad tracks in the Saturday afternoon serial at the Paramount Theater.

"Just wait right there," he said, his voice all raspy. "It'll take a while for you to get numb. We're going to get a little office work done while we're waiting." With that, they were gone, a whiteout in a blizzard, blowing into the adjoining room—to do some office work. Some very noisy office work. If only my ears were as numb as my face.

Oh, yeah! My childhood dental experiences had all the elements of a good horror story. It wasn't quite *Marathon Man,* but there was pain, dread, suspense, and the scariest of villains. I never told my parents about this episode that had escalated to such a frenzied … climax. But I do know that had it been a movie, it wouldn't have made it onto the short list my mother deemed suitable for her daughters—a list that banned *The Three Stooges.*

By the time I turned eleven, I refused to return to Needleman's office. I had a theory that novocain was responsible for my less-than-stellar school performance, but of course, my mother wasn't buying it.

When I became a teenager, Mom got a job as secretary/bookkeeper in a dental office, and our family switched to that practice.

The first time he examined me, my new dentist shook his head. "My, my, you've had a lot of work done, Peggy. Who was your dentist?"

When I told him, he groaned—ever so quietly.

One afternoon in high school while waiting for the bus with my friend Jeannie, the subject of teeth came up. I made the comment, "I had the worst dentist in the world!"

"Oh no, you didn't!" she said. *"I did!"*

We swapped horror stories about unnecessary fillings and needles—and the behind-the-chair and back-room escapades. Our dentists were one in the same, of course. Jeannie's father wasn't a Lion, and their family left the practice long before we did. Her parents had a more heightened sense of humor than mine, however, and had come up with a nickname of their own after hearing their daughter's stories: Dr. Drill-and-Fill.

I was naive for my age, and it would be a while before I fully appreciated the humor.

Chapter 3

HERE I COME!

IN 2001, MY HUSBAND AND I TRADED OUR COUNTRY home of almost forty years for a condo in a modern, four-story brick building with an elevator. There were no gardens to weed, no outdoor furniture to paint, and no more domestic diversions except cooking and occasional cleaning. After we were settled, there would be time to pursue my passion, and I would have a brand-new start.

I wanted to scream, *"Here I come, writing world!"* It was almost that simple.

On the advice of my husband, and on a downsizing frenzy, I threw away those folders bulging with rejection notices. There's only so much room in a condominium, after all. Besides, who wants to clutter their new home with reminders of inadequacy and failure? I might have kept one or two of the more encouraging ones. The ones that told me my writing showed promise, but that my story wasn't a good fit for their short list. I did keep one slip from a Maryland publisher who had simply stamped my query letter with a neat circle that contained the message, "Sorry, not at this time. Try again." So efficient. No needless words or time wasted on an encouraging message to a hopeful writer.

We had the choice of a condo in the back of the building that faced a field and woods or in the front— with a view of neighboring condos, a driveway, parking lot, and a trash corral. We hadn't yet made the decision when our son visited from out of town and weighed in.

"Definitely the unit in the front," he advised. "Lots of activity. You've seen enough rabbits and squirrels and deer. You'll enjoy the change. I can see you two now, eating at the kitchen table, your eyes glued to the front window watching people walking their dogs, traveling back and forth to the trash corral, bringing in the groceries. Dad sitting on the balcony and chatting. The two of you speculating about the neighbors...."

We took exception to his assessment of our frivolous lifestyle. We weren't nosey busybodies after all. But his little scenario did have appeal, and in the end we chose the front unit, and everything he had said was true. Our sunroom was the proverbial window on the world. And we spent hours speculating—about the young woman across the street and the suitability of her boyfriend; an elderly couple who seemed too frail to live on their own; and a man who seemed to wander the neighborhood aimlessly.

And boy, did we *know* stuff! Important stuff like who didn't break down their cardboard boxes before placing them in the trash corral; who didn't pick up after their dog; and who blew through the stop signs in the parking lot. Not that we would ever act on any of these infractions or spread tales. We were simply observers.

First and foremost, we were good neighbors. That day George slipped on ice and hit his head on the front sidewalk, my husband rushed to his aid. The morning Miss Anne was blown over by a strong gust of wind, we had just finished breakfast. John was at her side in a flash. And who could forget the afternoon Dolly tripped in the trash corral, broke her arm, and fractured a hip? When she refused to allow John to call 911, he and another neighbor put Dolly on a chair and carried her back to her unit. We found out later that she asked a friend to wash and curl her hair before calling 911. I would remind John of Dolly's story whenever he complained about me combing my hair or applying lipstick before taking our neighborhood walks.

Truth is, living in such a community was perfect for a writer. As our son had advised, we had been surrounded by nature and wildlife for decades. And now we were surrounded by people. As an observer of human behavior...well, let's just say there was no lack of material.

And because the writer in me can't *not write*, I continued telling stories, mostly about people and the memories they evoked, almost always seeing the humor.

I was delighted by the number of dogs in our new neighborhood and came to know them by name. The story below was my first in our new home. At the time, I had little hope of ever seeing it in print. Only my husband has read it. "It's a lot funnier now than it was back then," he said. I agreed.

"The Galloping Gourmet"

Day after day I watch our condominium neighbors walk their docile little dogs on leashes, from time to time allowing them to stop and sniff—a small, deceased rodent, or a bug, or worm, perhaps—only to be quickly snatched away from the offensive, disgusting object. I laugh to myself, wondering what the owner would think of our old dog, Shim.

Shim was the cutest puppy ever to chew up a checkbook or a TV remote or a rubber dental retainer. When you're adorable and affectionate, people are ever-so-patient while you outgrow those endearing puppy flaws.

Shim came to our family at the age of eight weeks—homeless, unwanted, and of undetermined breed. Our vet described her as a tan shepherd mix, which sounded classier than "mutt."

This tan shepherd mix shared our country home, enjoying not only the freedom of open fields, a flowing stream, and acres of woodland, but also an adoring entourage of two schoolteachers, three young boys, and six doting old neighbors. She galloped beside the horses, frolicked with the cat, chased rabbits and squirrels, raced to the bus stop to greet the kids after school, and loved everybody unconditionally.

Oh, yes—but for a few gastronomic quirks—our dog was the *perfect* pet, charming everyone she met, including cats and other dogs. Everybody agreed that our Shim was perfection on paws. That is, everybody who hadn't witnessed her disgusting, dark side.

Shim had an odd concept of food—more specifically, what *was* and what was *not* edible. I've known pets who were gourmets with such a highly developed palate, they would refuse to eat all but a certain brand of cat or dog food. Princess, my friend's cat, turned up her nose at beef and chicken, eating only fish and lamb—in gravy!

We once adopted a stray dog who refused to eat a bite unless she was alone. The minute someone stepped into the room, Ginger stopped eating, lifted her head, and growled. We figured she'd been abused and gave her space. And if her food wasn't room temperature, she wouldn't touch it. God forbid you should spruce up her kibble with some warm gravy or a slice of cold turkey from the fridge. Then there was Chip, my friend's elderly, temperamental Dalmatian, who would only eat food from a hand or a spoon. I kid you not!

Our Shim, on the other hand, was a foodie. Full-grown at sixty pounds, she was a connoisseur of anything that would fit into her mouth. Aside from dog chow, her four favorite food groups consisted of paper, animal waste, garbage, and any small wildlife she could outrun. Her paper of choice was the kind typically found in trash baskets—preferably the bathroom trash basket—in particular used tissue or feminine hygiene products. She loved nothing better than settling down on the living

room carpet in front of company to enjoy her carryout—
kind of like the kids loved settling down on the sofa with
a big bowl of popcorn while they enjoyed *The Brady
Bunch* or *M*A*S*H*. More than once, guests recoiled
in horror as my husband and I dragged Shim from the
room while prying open her incisors and shouting, "Bad
dog! Drop it!"

Her garbage fix came from the can in the backyard,
not to mention the plentiful small game in the woods
and fields surrounding our home. That was evident
from her engorged belly when she had feasted on such
forbidden bounty. She was relegated to her outdoor pen
on those occasions—although there were times when
our guard was down and her "catch of the day" appeared
in a steamy mound on our living room carpet.

I know what you're thinking: *You were foolish to allow
her to run free!* That's true perhaps, but it was a different
time—a time before leash laws. We lived in the country
with open spaces, horses, ponies, cats, woods, and a
stream. She was a great companion on trail rides. As I've
said, she was so darned lovable.

Shim embraced country life and considered the
horses her benefactors—and in truth, they were
exactly that. Our pasture was the equivalent of a 24/7
open buffet on a cruise ship where manure was the
daily special. As far as Shim was concerned, the fresher,
the better. It wasn't so bad in the winter when the
horses' droppings reflected their diet of grain and dry
hay. It was a different story in the summer when the
pasture grass was green and succulent. Of course, we
discouraged such behavior, but it was a losing battle.
She enjoyed all animal waste. I personally saw her

devour rabbit and fox scat. Another favorite activity was cleaning out the cat's litter box.

Early on, our dog developed a taste for the rats and mice that were drawn to the horses' sweet feed in the tack room. She was as formidable a hunter as any rat terrier and ready to pounce the minute a bale of hay or feed barrel was moved aside to reveal a rodent.

Shim greeted the farrier like he was Santa Claus and waited patiently as he clipped and filed the horses' hooves. She gnawed and devoured hoof clippings with the same enthusiasm she showed for ham and beef bones.

Oh, yes, the horses gave and gave where our dog was concerned but never as much as they did on that warm June morning in 1976—the day our veterinarian gelded two colts in our neighbor's pasture just across the narrow dirt lane.

An event of this magnitude didn't happen every day, mind you. In fact, this occurrence ranked right up there with the birth of Lady's filly in the front field down by the road. Word had spread like wildfire that the Conrad's palomino mare was about to foal, and curious people came running from far and near to witness the miracle of Mother Nature.

They came bearing apples, carrots, and sugar cubes—not unlike the wise men who brought gold, frankincense, and myrrh to the baby Jesus. The gallery cheered Lady on—from a respectable distance, of course—and practically cried when she licked the veil that covered the lovely foal. They actually did cry as the cream-colored filly struggled onto wobbly legs beside her mother.

And now, on this lovely June morning, our neighbors, with grandchildren and lawn chairs in tow—and fortified with bottles of beer—came to the paddock in the lower pasture to witness two colts losing their manhood.

It was a show all right, and I stared with laserlike focus—with Shim at my side. The experienced vet anesthetized the first colt and walked him in small circles until he crumpled gently to the ground. The vet was lightning fast at sterilizing the site, making two small incisions, and removing the testicles. Shim looked on with the intensity of a home plate umpire in the ninth inning of a tied World Series game.

It was what transpired next that has been seared in my memory over these past forty-five years. The veterinarian picked up the testes and casually slung them high over the fence and stream toward the gravelly, adjacent shore.

Shim was off like a shot, darting down the bank and across the water. John has since claimed that she caught the flying treat in midair. I don't remember it quite like that, but either way, she gobbled the tasty testicles to mixed reviews from the lawn chair gallery. Then our dog stood like an outfielder anticipating another fly ball.

The vet quickly reprised his performance on the second colt. And, yes, Shim's patience was rewarded minutes later to a chorus of horrified gasps.

From time to time I think about sharing this story with my condo neighbors whose pets consider the occasional doggie biscuit the ultimate treat.

Like I say: Shim might not have been the perfect dog, but we thought no less of her and counted our blessings. Luckily for us, she was not a face licker.

Chapter 4

SLUSH PILE 101

THERE ARE FEW ACTIVITIES MORE REWARDING THAN time spent with like-minded people. My cousin Nancy takes every opportunity to paint in the great outdoors with other *plein air* artists while an instructor looks over their shoulders. Son Scott, my fantasy enthusiast, has enjoyed gaming and sci-fi/fantasy conventions. My friend Pat spends time with her quilting and stitching groups whenever she has a chance. For me, it's writers' workshops and conferences.

The writing community has inspired me to write better. I've been encouraged to write every day, which is easy; it's being sidetracked from writing that's frustrating. I've learned to allow myself to write poorly. The important thing is to get it down; the real writing is in revision. I've been told to study writers I admire. One has only to look at my bookshelves to know that I've taken that advice. It's fun to hear successful authors talk about their office walls being papered with rejection notices from the early days. Author David Sedaris wrote every day for fifteen years before he was published. Even J. K. Rowling had her share of rejection letters.

When we were finally settled in our new condominium, John offered to drive me to the daylong book fair that was sponsored by Random House—where I would probably be hearing the usual encouraging words: "Remember, the only difference between a published writer and an unpublished writer is *persistence*. Believe in yourself! Do not give up!" One presenter at a previous conference had added as an aside, "But don't be delusional."

Whatever that meant.

On the morning of the book fair, I awoke early with a sense of exhilaration—kind of like that day I had learned that our youngest *would* be graduating from high school after all. And like the day our college student put aside his Dungeons & Dragons playbook and black jacket with the gold fire-breathing dragon, put on a school T-shirt, and picked up—gulp—a textbook!

At sixty-two, I had traversed that black abandoned mine of rejection and cancer and was ready to be a serious writer.

The sun had broken through the clouds, and I was *finally* taking charge of my life. They had a saying at the support group that we all tried to live by: don't sweat the small stuff. I liked the new me! After years of being a pleaser, I now had the guts to say to friends, "No, thank you! I've sat through my last 'home party!' Life is too short, and I don't need one more piece of Tupperware or jewelry or kitchen gadget."

Things had fallen into place at home as well. The boys were on their own, my husband was immersed in a life of volunteerism, and I had come to terms with reality. I would never be as slim as my sister or as domestic as Martha Stewart or as prolific as Erma Bombeck, with fifteen books and four thousand newspaper columns. And that was okay. It was 2002—a decade filled with promise.

I was glad that John was driving me to the daylong conference as it was forty miles away and I dislike highway driving. Plied with reading material and snacks, my patient husband took me to Carroll Community College. After a goodbye hug in the lobby, he wished me well and headed off for a walk around the spacious campus.

Random House had also sponsored a poetry contest. Winners would be announced at the end of the conference, and their poems would be published in a magazine. I knew that my silly little poem would never measure up to those strife-filled, angst-laden, sentimental, syrupy sweet poems that are so popular. It didn't have words such as *wispy clouds, ethereal glow,* or *tremulous, tormented souls.* I didn't stand a chance of winning, but it was fun to get back in the groove.

The presenter at this conference was a young editor from a major New York publishing house—one where I had submitted my book manuscripts, unsuccessfully. Slim, stylish, and businesslike, she spoke fast and had a persistent dry cough—the kind I get a day or so before coming down with a bad cold.

Her topic was the perennial "How to Get Published," and the room was filled with hopefuls—most of them young, but some middle-aged and older like me, busily taking notes that would hopefully lead to a publishing contract.

Her message was simple: if you are going to send a manuscript, always specify a particular editor by name in your submission *and* get the recommendation of an author represented by the house. "Otherwise, your manuscript is destined for the *slush pile,*" she warned, without a trace of sympathy. At previous conferences, presenters had looked us square in the eye and told us, "Some of our greatest finds have come from the slush pile."

"Let me tell you about something we call Pizza Slush Night," the young woman said with a maniacal gleam in her eye. "On the last Friday of the month, all editors are required to attend Pizza Slush Night, where we gather around a long table with pizza and soda. On the floor at the end of the table is the slush pile." She held out her arm, indicating a height of about four feet.

"Our goal is to address each of the submissions in that pile by the end of the evening. It's an assembly line, and here's how it works: The first person on either side of the table takes an envelope, opens it, and passes it along to the next, who removes the contents. The next person puts the cover letter and SASE on the top and passes it on. In the end, a rejection form letter is put into the SASE, and it is sealed. The original envelope and manuscript are dropped onto a discard pile at the other end of the table—unread—unless the sender indicates he wants his manuscript returned and has included a large, self-addressed stamped envelope. That requires an extra step in the assembly line."

Here, the young presenter paused for laughter. There was none.

As she concluded her presentation in a room that seemed devoid of oxygen, the only other sound to be heard was her hacking cough. If shock and dismay had an odor, the stench would have been overwhelming.

I thought of those dozens of carefully prepared book manuscripts I had printed and carried to the post office—like a naïve child sending a letter off to the North Pole and settling in for the long-anticipated Christmas morning. I thought of the form rejection letters that had filled my bulging folders. The ones that told me "After careful consideration, your story isn't the right fit for our needs." The ones that encouraged me to keep writing when in reality my manuscripts were destined for the slush pile. The wasted paper, ink, postage, and trips to the mailbox. And the tears.

Just that morning in another class, an editor had assured us, "A rejection means that your work simply isn't what that editor or publisher is looking for at that time." Another said, "A rejection means that your story isn't ready. It needs more work and time. After all, you don't want your writing out there if it isn't the very best it can be, do you? Imagine years later seeing your inferior work on the shelf—and feeling embarrassed."

It was a loss of innocence for sure and too much to comprehend! All from a presenter who had ignored the primary rule for writers everywhere—*know your audience*. My cruel side imagined the hacking editor at home the following day with laryngitis.

I felt as though I were trapped in an episode of *The Twilight Zone*, and when the feeling returned to my legs, I fled the room with one aim: to find my husband and escape. I had attended my last conference. There was no new advice, no pearls of wisdom I hadn't already heard. It meant nothing!

"What's wrong?" John asked, springing from his chair in the lobby. "You look like you've just witnessed a bludgeoning."

"Worse!" I said. "I'm ready to go."

"Why? What happened?"

"I'll tell you on the way home."

"What about your poem? The poetry contest?"

"Not interested. It's probably in a trash can somewhere."

"Look, I drove forty miles to get here—that's eighty miles worth of gas, and we're getting our money's worth! Come on, hon, I'll go with you."

With a heavy heart, I took his hand, and together we made our way to the Random House Media Center where we were stopped at the door. A man looked at my nametag, smiled, and handed me a magazine called *Into the Blue*.

"Congratulations!" he said. "Your poem made me laugh."

John and I looked at each other (I might have shivered just a little) and then made a beeline to the closest chairs where we opened the magazine. Sure enough, there it was—in the Humorous Poetry category. An international contest with hundreds, maybe *thousands* of entries—and my silly little poem was a winner!

The emcee spoke, then asked the winners to come to the front one at a time and read their poems. John and I listened as writers in the Serious Poetry category shared their work—earnest, sincere, sentimental writing, sometimes deep, and not always easy to follow. When it was time for the humorous poetry category, I told my husband there was no way I was going to get up in front of all those writers to read a poem that could have been written by a junior high student. But, of course, my chauffer had other ideas.

"You know what this means, right?" he asked.

"Yep. It means they are going to clap politely when I'm through and roll their eyes. John, you've heard their kind of poetry. It's in another class."

"Hey, the judges liked your poem. You're a published author, hon! Look at this magazine, published by one of the largest houses in the world. Now get up there and read your silly poem! With feeling—eighty miles worth!"

I made my way to the front of the room holding *Into the Blue*. I thanked the sponsors and told the audience that my poem was unlike the others. "It rhymes!" I said, laughing. "And it's pure fantasy." And then I read my silly poem...with feeling...eighty miles worth!

Too Real

My husband is an artist,
His work has great appeal.
Though objects in his paintings,
Are frequently too real.

Our walls are filled with artwork,
It's hanging everywhere.
But sometimes it's so lifelike,
It gives me quite a scare.

A landscape scene with oak trees,
Hangs near the hallway door.
Each fall when it gets chilly,
Acorns litter the floor.

A still-life's in the kitchen,
A bowl of grapes and cheese.
For some strange, eerie reason,
It draws fruit flies and bees.

He painted me a rooster,
So, it comes as no surprise,
That now we never sleep late,
It's with the sun we rise.

His portrait of Houdini
Once hung behind his chair.
It disappeared last winter,
Just vanished in thin air!

A watercolor folk art,
Gives our foyer atmosphere.
A barnyard scene with cattle,
Some pigs, some sheep, a steer.

The cows are grazing calmly,
The calves are full of pep.
Next time you come to visit,
Be careful where you step!

There were chuckles as I read, then laughter, and finally, applause. My writing had never drawn applause. Afterward, other writers asked me to sign my poem in their books. The laughter and applause stayed in my head for a long time, kind of like a favorite tune you can't stop hearing. In fact, I could still hear it at the Bob Evans restaurant where we stopped for a celebratory dinner on the way home following the daylong roller-coaster ride.

But we didn't linger over our meal. I kept thinking about the magazine Elizabeth had brought to me. I had to get home and write a horse story!

Chapter 5

AND WRITE, I DID!

MOST OF THE CONFLICTS IN OUR HOME WERE THE result of books. How many times were my sons late to the table because of a book? Or didn't get enough sleep because of a book? Or negligent about chores because of a book? I heard my family's pleas and excuses in my sleep: "Just one more page before I turn out the light, Mom. I promise ... I meant to do my homework, but I had to finish my library book. I knew you wouldn't want to pay a fine." Even my husband was famous for saying, "Just one more chapter, hon, then we'll leave; it's a short one." He was also famous for monopolizing the bathroom because of a book—and still is.

The truth is, I envy my husband and the sons I describe as voracious readers. Even as toddlers, the children walked around clutching their favorite books, hoping to catch their father or me relaxing. Some books I had read to them so many times, they'd been memorized. It was impossible to return from our weekly grocery shopping without a new Golden Book. Later, my husband and I were vigilant about the reading material in our home— knowing that it would likely be read by the boys. To this day, John can have as many as three books "going" at a time. When it comes to bonding with the boys, his favorite topic is his latest good read.

It was one of the messages I heard over and over in my writing courses: "If you want to be a writer, you must be a reader! Not just because it helps us to understand human nature, but because we learn to love language through reading. More importantly, it expands our imagination." According to Stephen King, "Reading is the creative center of a writer's life." And who could forget William Faulkner's advice to writers: "Read, read, read. Read everything—trash, classics, good and bad, and see how they do it. Just like a carpenter who works as an apprentice and studies the master. Read! You'll absorb it."

Unfortunately, that was not great news for this writer. I wondered if it was even possible for a self-described slow reader to be a serious writer. Slow as in, I can't keep up with the captions at the bottom of the TV screen. Oh,

I've read countless worthwhile books and even some fine literature. And I've certainly known the pleasure of curling up with a good book. In more recent years, I've spent hours reading and studying long-admired humor writers. But for me, reading has always been a ponderous exercise. "Could a person be a serious writer with such a handicap?" I wondered. And then there was the matter of my idyllic life.

In 2002, *Seabiscuit* was still all the rage. As a lover of horses, I couldn't put it down. As a writer, I was fascinated by the fact that author Laura Hillenbrand had suffered from chronic fatigue syndrome since 1987 when she was twenty years old. She endured severe vertigo and exhaustion that left her incapacitated and housebound for many years. That this writer was able to persevere *and* produce a best-seller seemed nothing short of miraculous.

Laura Hillenbrand joined a long list of well-known authors who have struggled to overcome hardship. Margaret Mitchell once famously said, "Hardships make or break people." Her first husband had taken off after only four months of marriage, never to be seen again. When she suffered complications from a broken ankle, her career as a journalist ended abruptly. So she set about writing *Gone with the Wind*, a little novel about the Civil War and reconstruction. It took three years to write and earned her a Pulitzer Prize.

Elizabeth Barrett Browning suffered with debilitating physical ailments from an early age, as did Ernest Hemingway. He committed suicide at the age of fifty-seven—after writing a mere twenty-five books. When J. K. Rowling's marriage ended and she was left penniless, jobless, and depressed, she, too, had considered suicide—and went on to write a masterpiece. Robert

Louis Stevenson, Tennessee Williams, and Stephen King battled addiction.

Even the beloved Erma Bombeck was diagnosed with an incurable, untreatable genetic disease when she was twenty years old. She survived breast cancer and a mastectomy and endured daily dialysis.

Dealing with breast cancer when I was middle-aged helped me to relate to others with illness. But really, it was my only brush with adversity. While growing up, my greatest hardships had been living with a perfect sister and without a pony. And having to endure base-ball games where my mother shouted obscenities at the umpires and danced in the aisles at the stadium. In short, I had led a life of privilege—with good health.

Nevertheless, write, I did. This slow reader—who had never known the heartbreak of domestic discord, the tragedy of addiction, life with an incurable illness, or extreme poverty, and who had no market for her work— wrote every day. Because the writer within had no choice. There were stories to tell. Stories about the people in my life. People I loved and admired, people whose behavior I didn't always understand, and people who made me laugh. Because what writer does not long to have their work read by someone? Anyone? And appreciated?

Two loving, supportive parents who were my cheer-leaders until the day they died were a great asset to my writing life. They presented me with two of my earliest opportunities to share my prose on the occasions of their ninetieth and ninety-first birthdays in 2002.

On the calendar, the two events took place within one month—but on a celebration scale, they were light years apart. By the time my husband and I were settled in our condo, Mom and Dad had moved into a senior living facility just minutes away. My sister and I planned a ninetieth birthday bash there for Mom, but not all family members were able to attend. I wrote the following story so they could at least celebrate vicariously and not miss the full scope of what happened.

"An Affair to Remember— On the Occasion of Mom's Ninetieth Birthday"

Exhausted, I pushed my mother's wheelchair through the mall and plopped down on a bench in front of Friendly's Restaurant. "Well, Mom, we've tried Lord & Taylor, Macy's, and Hecht's. Let's take a break and have a sandwich."

It was 2002, and Mom was in pursuit of the perfect outfit for her ninetieth birthday celebration. Something that would "wow" her friends and neighbors and relatives. In years past, she'd have whipped up an original creation on her old Singer sewing machine. She knew a thing or two about fashion and quality and wasn't about to "settle." Her expectations were modest—something well-constructed, understated, classy, and not too expensive. She was ninety, after all, and she reminded me, "How many more opportunities will I have to wear a 'dressy' outfit?"

The expensive dress she had tried on at Macy's had given us a rare opportunity to share some humor. Mom was usually too busy taking charge to appreciate the lighter side of things.

"Hmm ... it's expensive, but you can bury me in this," she said, looking in the dressing room mirror. "That way I'll get my money's worth. How does it look in the back?"

I went out on a limb. "Who cares? It's for your burial," I said with a straight face. "Nobody's going to see it." She smiled at me in the mirror as we shared a little unspoken humor. My mother and I were the same size, and she knew darn well there was no way this lovely dress was going underground. Our tastes were different, but I always knew where to look on those rare occasions I needed something elegant—Mom's closet never disappointed. Minutes later, she announced that she couldn't justify the expense, and we moved on.

"No," Mom said glancing up at the red-and-white Friendly's sign. "I have to get back to your father. Miss Ruth can only stay with him until three o'clock. We still have two more big stores, then there are a couple of smaller shops we haven't tried. Besides, I'm not even tired." She pointed the way to JCPenney, warning, "Be careful of that bump at the entrance, Peggy. That last one nearly gave me whiplash."

We had been at it for the past two hours, and I was tempted to tell her, "Mom, lower your expectations a little!" But when had I ever actually spoken my mind to my mother? When I reminded her that she had a closet full of lovely, custom-made outfits, her response was, "Oh, your father has seen me in those old things so many times. I need something new!"

My father was blind—and had been for ten years.

Had Norman Rockwell been there, he'd have set up an easel and reached for his brushes—a senior woman pushing a wheelchair while her ancient mother pointed the way ahead like an explorer who had just spotted land. All the while being passed by energetic young people looking as if they were working on their ten thousand daily steps.

After another hour of shopping, unsuccessfully, Mom said, "You know, I'm still not tired. Sometimes I wonder if I really do have congestive heart failure. Okay, honey, let's try those smaller shops."

In the end, she couldn't find anything as classy as the outfits hanging in her own closet. She looked at me and with a straight face said, "This has been a waste of time. At least we got our exercise."

After a mere four hours, I pushed Mom to the car, then made my way back to the wheelchair corral in the mall, making a mental note: if my mother needed a new outfit to celebrate her hundredth birthday, my sister, Janet, could do the honors.

That evening Jan came in from Richmond, and the following day she and I visited the party planner / caterer at the retirement home where Mom and Dad resided. We carried a list because, naturally, Mom had planned every detail—guest list, menu, drinks, music, and speakers.

"Mom," we reasoned, "why don't you just go with us? You know exactly what you want."

"And let them think I've planned my own party?! How would that look?"

So two dutiful, loving daughters sighed and headed down the corridor, list in hand. I had made a photo collage and ordered a tasteful arrangement of flowers (pastel, as requested) with a matching corsage. Hopefully, they would meet with our mother's approval. The leading character in our birthday production would be my mother, naturally, but an essential supporting character was the birthday cake. On our list, the specifications were underlined in red: White icing! Pale pink roses! And pale green leaves. Nothing bright or gaudy!

Tasteful pastel to match the flower arrangement and her corsage.

It was a lovely party, held in the elegant Garden Room, surrounded by tall windows looking out on lovely bushes and trees and fall flowers. The weather was perfect, and everyone came, including a half dozen or so of Mom's Virginia relatives. At the podium, I welcomed guests and introduced family members, then Mike shared a lighthearted poem about his grandmother. She listened with interest, nodding in approval from time to time. Scott roamed the room with a video camera on his shoulder capturing all the action. Phil took charge of the music. When he had suggested having a karaoke machine and encouraging guests to entertain as well, his grandmother turned quite pale, fanned herself, and raised her eyebrows until they disappeared.

Guests were enjoying three kinds of dainty sand-wiches that afternoon, along with punch and coffee—when it happened.

"We're ready for the cake," my sister told the head waitress.

"What cake?" the woman said. "There is no cake. No cake was ordered."

"Well, of course we ordered a cake."

Feeling our mother's eyes scrutinizing the exchange from across the room, Jan and I were careful not to show the panic we felt. The waitress pulled a paper from her pocket and confirmed that, indeed, no cake had been ordered. We had talked about it, but apparently moved on to something else before actually placing the order. Oh, no....

"We assumed you were bringing in your own dessert. People sometimes do that," the waitress said.

The room went suddenly dark and fuzzy. Conversations blurred, and the words "major coronary" ran through my mind. Fortunately, my sister was there. As the oldest, she was in charge—I'm pretty sure of that. So the buck would stop in her capable hands.

"So," Janet said, putting her hands on her cheeks, "you mean that not only is there no cake but there is no dessert at all? Of any kind?"

"Oh @#$%!" one of us might have uttered (I'm sure I don't recall just who …). "What are we going to do?"

And that's when a blur raced across the corner of my vision—two angels, actually.

"What's wrong, Mom?" my daughter-in-law Marjie, asked as Cousin Nancy whispered a frantic shriek, "Peggy, what's the matter? You look like you're going to pass out."

So we told them, and before we finished, Nancy asked, "Where's the closest grocery store?"

"There's a Food Lion right across the street…." Before I could finish, Nancy and Marjie were flying through the door, purses in hand. I shouted after them, "White icing with pastel pink roses … nothing gaudy!"

Our mother smelled trouble, so while waitresses scoured freezers in the various dining rooms for left-over desserts from Sunday lunch, Janet assured her that things were fine—just a tiny glitch. Not for the first time, I found myself wishing that my sister lived nearby instead of two hundred miles away. A half hour later, guests had barely delved into the assortment of partially thawed leftover slices of pie when Marjie and Nancy returned to the party—followed by a waitress carrying a lovely sheet cake.

If Mom noticed the bright red, blue, and green decorations on the cake, she chose not to mention it. Or maybe she was just too busy basking in tributes from friends, and a slightly off-key rendition of "Happy Birthday." I learned later that there was only one other cake available—a sheet cake with the message *Happy Retirement, Uncle Bud.*

Nancy and Marjie had chosen well.

Mom looked lovely in her vintage silk blouse and homemade skirt and managed to stay out of her wheelchair for the entire party. When Dad told her she looked beautiful in her new outfit, she kissed him on the forehead. As usual, his face turned red.

All in all, it was a delightful party. Jan and I decided that if we're around for our ninetieth birthdays, we'll settle for cake and ice cream.

Mom's family loved reading the story, even the ones who had attended the party. They said that I had "captured Thelma [their sister and aunt] to a T."

My father had always disliked parties and could usually be found observing the action from a safe distance in a comfortable chair. The fact that he could no longer see and was still willing to be on display, on the front lines so to speak, is a testament to his love and devotion to my mother.

"An Afternoon to Remember"

We had scarcely recovered from my mother's ninetieth birthday party four weeks earlier when my father turned ninety-one. Mom respected his request for a quiet observance. After all, she had forced him to endure a houseful of company and speeches a year earlier for his ninetieth. And then again for her ninetieth. For the last ten years of his life, Dad had been blind and weak from a stroke. Several days a week while Mom ran errands or played a game of bridge with friends, I sat with him, asking questions like an inquisitive newspaper reporter and taking notes as he relived his boyhood in a nearby neighborhood.

On his ninety-first birthday, I brought him home-made chocolate brownies with peanut butter icing—his favorite—and a book of poetry. An odd choice, some might argue, for a blue-collar tradesman with a seventh-grade education who had never read a book. While Mom took a well-deserved break, Dad and I reclined on twin beds snacking on grapes and brownies. I opened a book and began reading a passage from *The Song of Hiawatha* when suddenly, I heard his voice. I stopped reading and listened as he recited from memory:

"Dark behind it rose the forest,
Rose the black and gloomy pine trees..."

When he faltered, I resumed reading, and again, he joined in. Innately intelligent, Dad had always been the go-to person for math problems, repairs of any kind, and common-sense advice. But poetry? Never!

"I guess I remember it from school," was his explanation. It had been almost eighty years since he'd finished the seventh grade. I turned the page to another Longfellow poem:

"Under the spreading chestnut tree,
The village smithy stands..."

Again, Dad joined in; again, I stopped reading and he continued.

"The smith a mighty man is he,
With large and sinewy hands..."

How incredible that I could have known this perfect father and husband for more than sixty years and never heard him recite these poems? How touching that a twelve-year-old boy had been so moved by these lines as to memorize them. Really! Teachers don't always know how they are influencing students.

Until that day, I hadn't shared my own creative writing with Dad. On some level, I was probably ashamed that it wasn't good enough to be published. Oh, he knew that I dabbled in writing. But when I told him about the book fair just weeks earlier and placed my copy of "Into the Blue" in his hands, he caressed the booklet, as if it were his treasured Bible—the one presented to him by the church he had attended most of his life.

I opened it and read my nonsense poem on "realism" aloud, and Dad laughed. So I shared some other poems with my captive audience—poems I had written for young children years ago and put aside.

Dad shook his head after each and asked, "Did you really write that?" When I finished, he said, "They sound like poems you would read in a fancy poetry book! Maybe someday you'll write a book, hon!"

My simple children's poems that brightened Dad's ninety-first birthday are still among my favorites. Dad especially loved this one:

I Think I'll Run Away

I'm sick and tired of living here,
My family's mean to me.
I'm not allowed to dig a hole,
Or climb high in a tree.

My father hid his tools from me,
The hammer and the saw.
How can I nail things to the floor?
Or decorate the wall?

My mother makes me pick up toys,
And brush my teeth each day.
And wash my hands before I eat.
I think I'll run away!

I'll pack some cookies in a bag,
A flashlight for the dark.
I'll leave my soap and toothbrush home,
And move into the park.

I'll take a coat for wintertime,
Galoshes for my feet.
I won't be going too far, I'm not…
Allowed to cross the street.

John and I joined Mom and the birthday boy for supper that evening. Afterwards, Dad asked me to reread my poems and claimed that it was the nicest birthday he could remember. I had no doubt that this was the best part of being a writer—seeing the wonder and pride in the face of one I so admired. I'd grown up in a time before parents told their kids "I love you" every hour of the day. When it came to love, my mother and father used the most relevant technique employed by good writers everywhere: "Show it—don't tell it." And that's precisely what they did—every day—for the sixty-seven years I knew them.

Chapter 6

AT LAST!

"HI, PEGGY. IT'S JOHN. YOUR MOM TELLS ME YOU'VE been published in the *Saturday Evening Post*!" our long-time minister and friend said. "I had to call and congratulate you!"

"Don't I wish!" I said. "I was a winner in their limerick contest, that's all. Five lines that describe a cartoon. It's not a big deal."

"Still ... your limerick must have been better than hundreds of others! Hang in there, Peg. One of these days...."

Church friends were especially supportive and always asking where they could read my work. "It's still on my computer," I'd tell them, smiling. From time to time, I would write a letter to the editor of the newspaper. If it was published, church ladies would cut it out and bring it to Sunday School or Bible study or the women's circle meetings—where they would read it aloud to the group.

It was 2003, and my mother was constantly on the prowl for bragging material. She lived in a retirement community with over a thousand residents and having a daughter who was published in a *real* magazine would give her a nice competitive edge. None of her friends' children were successful writers.

Not that she wasn't already proud of me—I was just a child when she first explored the possibility of my becoming a writer. Apparently, I was famous for my somewhat fanciful stories.

"Peggy has an active imagination," she would tell people. When I was in the first grade, I was invited to tell stories after lunch. Every day I stood before twenty to thirty kids and made up a story *off the top of my head.* Mom and Mrs. Harrison, my teacher, were church friends, and enjoyed many a laugh over those stories—after Mom was reassured that they were pure fiction and not family secrets. Later, when I would come into the house after a day of rounding up cattle on my pretend horse, I would share my incredible experiences with my mother. Instead of telling me to quit lying, she would smile and say that maybe I would be a writer one day.

A few months earlier I had taken Elizabeth's advice and written and submitted a short, humorous story for an international horse publication. As time passed, I forgot about it and began writing articles and short stories to submit to other horse magazines.

And then came that morning when I sat at my computer and learned that I had actually sold my first short story. As I've said, I'm not partial to phrases such as, *The heavenly angels sang the Hallelujah Chorus,* but I did call my mother—my biggest cheerleader—even before I told the children. Mourning the loss of my father after seventy years of marriage had left her depressed, and I was anxious to share some good news. She didn't mind one bit being awakened at 6 a.m. Her silence upon hearing my news that morning was louder than any praise, and I knew that she was catching her breath.

"Oh, honey," Mom said when she had found her voice. "I'm as proud as punch! Are they going to pay you? Will they print your name on the story? Did you send them a picture? You should always do that."

Being published didn't seem real until that day the magazine, along with a check for fifty dollars, appeared in our mailbox. It was Wednesday, March 3, 2004, to be exact, and you'd have thought we had won the Publishers Clearing House sweepstakes.

It was finally the beginning of my professional career. I was sixty-six, and for the occasion, my husband and I pulled out all the stops and celebrated at the Golden Corral for the early bird senior special.

It seems like just yesterday—John sitting across the table reading my story aloud, from time to time laughing as though he were reading it for the first time, and reaching over to squeeze my hand ever so gently. Of course, he had already read it aloud to me so that I could hear how it sounded before sending it off. It looked so official in print, with a picture even! And my name at the top just beneath the title, "Competition."

Seeing my husband holding a magazine containing *my* story validated me as a writer somehow. People were paying money to read my fictional story about a teenage boy with a crush on a horse-crazy girl! John smoothed the page carefully as he read, reminding me of the way Dad had caressed *Into the Blue* from the book fair. I felt that if I never sold another story, it was OK. My mother was proud, and my kids were happy for me. John claimed to be "not a bit surprised," but you could tell it was a big deal. We'd been at the Golden Corral twenty minutes and hadn't even gotten in the buffet line.

A friend advised me to open a bank account in my name. "Earning your own money will make you feel independent, Peggy," she said. "Give you some self-worth! And John will have a new respect for you." I smiled as though I might take her advice, but I knew better. That might work for some couples, and that's fine, but for us, all that we had was *ours*. As for respect…no problems there either.

Here is my first-ever published story that was responsible for our humble, though joyous, celebration.

"Competition"
(Horsey Humor) Fiction by Peggy Rowe
HORSE-Canada, 2004

Amanda Kellerman is a knockout. I've been trying all year to get to know her, but all she ever talks about is her horse. Last month she came to school with a nasty bruise on her upper arm. When I asked her what happened, she said, "My horse has a sweet nature, but sometimes he's a *little* temperamental."

It seems this sweet-natured horse bit her while she was tightening the thing that goes around his waist to hold the saddle in place. Not that I blame him. A week later, Amanda came to school on crutches. I overheard her telling a friend that while she was brushing dried mud from her horse's belly, he showed his appreciation by kicking her legs out from under her—a sign of gratitude in horse talk, apparently.

I realize that if I'm going to get to know this girl before her temperamental horse does her in, I'll have to learn to speak her language. So, I get a book from the library called, *Your Friend, The Horse*, or some such nonsense.

It's deadly dull, but I read enough to learn a few horsey terms. I figure it might help me get my foot in the stable door.

Monday morning there she is at her desk in homeroom, looking prettier than ever and still in one piece. This is where I impress the heck out of her.

"So …," I say casually, "is your horse a stallion or a gelding?"

Amanda looks at me as though she's never seen me before. "Cordy is a gelding. Stallions don't make good pleasure horses. They're too aggressive."

I try to remember another horsey term to throw at her, but I'm busy trying to imagine what Cordy might do to her if he were aggressive.

"Do you like horses too?" she asks me.

"Who doesn't like horses?" I lie. "But I'm involved in football right now."

"Football is so violent!" she says, frowning.

I glance at the fading bruise on her arm and laugh, thinking she's making a joke, but she isn't. "By the way," I say, changing the subject, "Cordy is an unusual name."

"It's short for Cordial."

I always thought cordial meant friendly and good-natured, but it must have another meaning: *bloodthirsty* or *murderous*. Just then, Amanda drops her notebook, and it flops open on the floor. I look down and notice the slipper on her right foot.

"Oh, that's nothing. Cordy accidently stomped on my foot last night when I was feeding him," she explains. "No broken bones, just some bruising and swelling."

Hmmm…maybe she's having second thoughts about "Mr. Temperamental Sweetness." This is my chance to step in. So, I pick up her notebook and see a drawing on the inside cover—a big red heart with the name Cordial printed in the center. *What am I missing here?* I decide to go out on a limb.

"Uhh, would you like to get together sometime?"

"Sure." And she smiles that beautiful smile. "You could come over to my place on Saturday. I'll introduce you to Cordy. He doesn't usually like guys, but maybe you'll be an exception. If he likes you, you can help me groom him. Then we could shovel manure together."

The bell rings so I hand her the notebook. "Uh, I'll see you later," I say and head for my seat. It's hard to concentrate while I'm staring at her long wavy ponytail. A guy just can't compete with a horse.

Then suddenly, it comes to me. Who needs horsey phrases? I'll just sneak up behind her in the hall this afternoon, and in a sweet-natured, temperamental way, chomp down on her arm. Then I'll kick her on the shin.

Yeah, that'll work. By tomorrow morning *my* name will be in a red heart on Amanda's notebook.

≪ ◆ ≫

Mom had a manic expression when she asked to borrow the magazine for a few days, as some of the church ladies would be visiting over the weekend. I knew it was destined for her coffee table where it would be the center of attention. As proud as she was, though, my ultimate writing gift to my mother was the article published in *Guideposts* magazine when she was ninety-three. It was about her devotion to the Baltimore Orioles and the day she threw out the opening pitch. That magazine traveled the halls of her retirement community in the pocket of her Rascal Scooter like a treasured companion.

I regretted that my parents never realized the full impact they had on my writing life, not to mention the parade of interesting characters who had marched through my childhood. Relatives, friends, and strangers gave me a window into human nature and the self-awareness that is so essential to writers.

Looking back on the summer little Mary came into my life is embarrassing. I saw her as a nuisance, an intrusion, and a threat to my position in the family, for sure. Writing about the summer of 1945 has not only revealed my childhood character flaws but has given me a brand-new appreciation for two parents who "walked the walk."

"The Longest Summer"

My mother made the announcement as she cleared the dinner table, making it sound as though it was no big deal. "By the way, Miss Ella has to go to the hospital for a while, so little Mary is going to spend a few days with us." This didn't seem unusual—someone coming to stay with us *wasn't* a big deal. It seemed there was always somebody—mostly relatives—using our spare bedroom.

Except that Miss Ella wasn't a relative—just a church friend—and she and Mom had never seemed particularly close. I should have been suspicious when Mom and Mary came through the front door the next day with two big suitcases for "just a few days." I'd seen the girl around Sunday school before, but at seven years old, I hadn't paid much attention to the little five-year-old. I definitely didn't remember her being so pretty.

Mom took me aside. "Peggy, we need to be especially kind to Mary. She's never been away from home before." Which meant she'd probably act like a little sister and follow me around. But that was okay as long as she didn't mess with my dog and my stuff. What's a few days when the whole glorious summer lay ahead?

"She'll sleep in your twin bed so Janet can help keep an eye on her and make her feel at home," Mom said. "You can have the spare room with the *big* bed all to yourself. You'll be like a guest. Won't that be fun?"

Wait a minute . . . sleep alone? My older sister and I had always shared the front bedroom, waking up to the cheerful morning sun pouring through two big windows.

"But … can we keep the door open? And the hall light on? Can Topper sleep with me?"

"Yes. Yes. And *no!* He'd be on your bed in a flash."

The mother of all cardinal rules in our house was, "No dogs on the furniture! No exceptions!" Not that Topper didn't sneak onto the sofa when Mom wasn't around. But he was smart enough to jump down when he heard her coming. Of course that was no assurance he wouldn't end up in the doghouse anyway after Mom checked the cushions for his body indentation and felt around for a warm spot.

So it began—the summer of sharing *my* home and *my* family with royalty and her precious little teddy bear.

The writing was on the wall that very first evening at dinner when the string beans were passed. "No, thank you," Mary said, as though a kid had a choice in our house. "I don't like green vegetables. Mommy doesn't make me eat them." I had to chuckle to myself; this was going to be fun.

You had to hand it to my mother, who had no wide-eyed, eyebrow-raising dramatics. She simply smiled and placed two beans on Mary's plate. "No one is going to *make* you eat anything, dear, but it would be nice if you would just taste them. They make you strong! There's a good girl," she said, reaching down to Mary's lap and giving Teddy a pat on the head.

Who *was* this syrupy stranger wearing my mother's checkered apron? Certainly not the same woman who spooned mountains of spinach and Brussels sprouts onto my plate, expecting me to eat every last leaf!

There was more of the same the next morning. "And what would you like for breakfast, honey?" I was reminded of the book my mother read to me when I was Mary's age, *The Little Princess*, where servants just couldn't do enough for the child who wanted for nothing. Meanwhile, my breakfast was plopped in front of me like Topper's bowl of kibble was plopped on the floor beneath the sink.

My mother's camera was never far away—usually in her apron pocket. You'd think Mary was her only child, and she had to document every fascinating moment of her childhood. *Click*. I couldn't remember ever being photographed eating vegetables ... or a breakfast waffle. Oh well, just a few more days.

At night I could hear my eleven-year-old sister and Mary talking in the bedroom next door. Sometimes Janet even read a story aloud as Mary hugged Teddy. She couldn't do enough for her royal highness—introducing her to bubble baths and teaching her to play simple tunes on the piano while Mom peeked around the corner. *Click*. Janet even allowed her to tag along when friends came over. It was Janet and Mary, Mary and Janet. *Click*. But I didn't care. I had my dog and my horse.

I can still see her sitting at my sister's feet in the evening looking every bit like Rapunzel as Janet brushed and braided her long blonde locks—instead of playing 500 Rummy with me. *Click*. She used to brush *my* hair when I was little—like I was her doll. Not that I would sit still for it now.

To make matters worse, this five-year-old was so darned sweet and good—just like the princess in the story. Of course, it was all an act with her never running through the house or screaming or getting bubble gum stuck in her hair. It wasn't normal.

I felt as if I could have run away from home that summer and not been missed. That is, until the wet dishes piled up with nobody to dry them and the garbage spilled onto the counter with nobody to carry it outside to the can. Huh! When dog droppings littered the backyard, I guarantee you there'd have been a search party.

And suddenly it was July, a whole month later, and guess who was still with us—and even more adored by her subjects, if that's possible. Her royal highness was now up to four string beans and a whole tablespoon of spinach. The night she ate one measly Brussels sprout, you'd have thought she had discovered penicillin—there was that much praise. The evening Mom served asparagus, she conspired with my sister ahead of time.

"Mmm . . . Mom, these little spears taste so buttery!" Janet raved. "I love them." It worked! Mary ate one whole spear. *Click!*

My mother knew what she was doing all right. Like our church's choir director, she was our leader—determining when we were too loud or needed to move along faster or slow down. She established the mood, all right, and prompted us when it was our turn to carry out a task.

When it came to the Fourth of July, I didn't even mention the big parade downtown. My father was no longer a fan. For the past two years, he had refused to take us, saying, "I don't want to get tied up with the parking and with all that parade traffic!"

I should have known better. All of a sudden it was, "Say hon, how about we take the children downtown to the Fourth of July parade in the morning?" I couldn't complain about this one. Parades were the best, with all those lovely horses—even if the princess was our reason for going.

Dad had been right about the traffic and the crowds. We had to park blocks away, then maneuver along the curb to find a spot where we could see the action. Except for Mary, of course. She had the best seat in the house, high above everyone else—*on my father's shoulders*—where I used to be, back in the days when I was young and cute. *Click.*

I thought back to when I was Mary's age, and my mother fell down the steps and broke her foot. I had been sent to stay with Aunt Cornelia, where I was homesick every minute of the day. My father came to visit me evenings after work. I sat on his lap and cried the entire time, and when he could bear it no more, he took me home with him.

"How come Mary's father never comes to see her?" I asked my mother.

"I thought you knew," my mother said, speaking in a low voice. "Mary's father died last year. He was sick for a long time. I guess I didn't tell you."

I was coming to terms with something akin to pity, and perhaps even a touch of guilt, when a scary thought popped into my narcissistic little brain. *What if Miss Ella died? Like the father of the Little Princess in the story? Only instead of Mary going to live in an orphanage, my parents adopted her? And she came to live with us—forever and ever? Adopting an orphan was just the sort of thing my parents would do.*

"I have a good idea, Peggy," my mother said the following morning. "It's a beautiful day; the sun is shining, and the birds are singing…Why don't you take Mary out back and introduce her to your horse? You could teach her to ride."

She was talking about my pretend horse, naturally—a cushion on top of the poles that supported the backyard grapevines, some clothesline for reins, and some old purses for saddlebags. We had no place to keep a real horse, even if we could afford one. Or, at least, that was the story repeated over and over by my parents—like the refrain of a never-ending hymn.

My mother named him Cordie after the Concord grapes that covered his body in the summer. Unlike real horses, who shed their coats in the spring, Cordie shed his grapes and leaves in the fall.

"A horse?!" Mary screamed, jumping up and down. "I didn't know you had a horse! I never rode a horse before! Where is it?" She took my hand—her new best friend—and together we went to the backyard by the alley where I helped her to mount my pretend horse. In a few weeks, the grapes would ripen, and Mary's clothes and legs would be stained purple. She sat there for a moment jiggling the reins before asking quite possibly the dumbest question ever.

"How do you make it go?"

I shook my head in disbelief and was about to tell her to drop a coin in the slot and push the button, when I saw my mother lurking about with her you-know-what. *Click!*

"He doesn't move," I said, trying to sound patient, in case … "He's an imaginary horse. Like your Teddy is an imaginary bear. Teddy doesn't growl, or bite you, or hibernate in the winter. Cordie doesn't move. You have to use your imagination, Mary!"

So I told her about riding the prairie and rounding up steers on a cattle drive. But really, this five-year-old had no more imagination than the wooden picnic table a few yards away. You almost have to feel sorry for somebody like that. Almost. It's hard to feel sorry for somebody who steals your bed and your family. Not to mention ruining summer vacation.

The greatest betrayal of all came in August. Mary had been with us so long that even Topper forgot she was just a visitor, and I worried again that her mother had died—and I'd be stuck with her forever.

I awoke extra early that morning, and on my way to the bathroom, I looked into my old bedroom awash in cheerful sunlight with the occupants sound asleep. That's when I saw him—my pal Topper—asleep on my bed beside Mary, her hand draped over his back as Teddy lay forgotten, facedown on the floor. I gasped quietly, resisting the urge to scream. Instead, I ran down the hall for my mother.

"Look at that!" I whispered with all the indignation I could muster. "I bet she fed him a cookie." I looked up at Mom. Surely the palace roof was about to fall on her Royal Highness.

But instead, my mother ran to her bedroom, and returned with ... *Click!* Then she reminded me that Mary would soon be leaving our home. It was music to my ears and couldn't happen soon enough.

I thought about calling my dog but was afraid that if he awoke now and saw my mother while he was on the bed, he would die of fright.

When the long-awaited day finally arrived, my sister and I carried Mary's suitcases to the car and rode along. Miss Ella, very much alive, greeted us at the door but had eyes only for her daughter. She wrapped her arms around Mary and cried—then cried some more as they sat together on the sofa rocking gently side to side.

Neighbors and a relative were visiting so we didn't stay, but as we were leaving, Mom handed Mary a photograph album.

"This is for you, Mary," she said. "You can show Mommy what you've been doing all summer."

"Look at this picture, Mommy," I heard her saying before the door closed behind us. "Peggy showed me how to ride her horse. He's imaginary—like Teddy. Oh, and I changed Teddy's name to Cordie ...."

I skipped to the car, noticing for the first time the sunshine and music from the birds—and feeling truly grateful that Miss Ella was alive.

Chapter 7

A NEW FRONTIER

Eʟɪᴢᴀʙᴇᴛʜ's ꜱᴜɢɢᴇꜱᴛɪᴏɴ ᴛᴏ ᴡʀɪᴛᴇ ᴀ ꜱᴛᴏʀʏ ꜰᴏʀ ᴀ horse magazine was spot on. Having been a horse enthusiast my entire life, I spoke the language with ease. I was merely exercising a quote usually attributed to Mark Twain: "Write what you know." What aspiring writer has not heard that advice?

Sadly, arthritis intruded into my longtime passion for horses. When I could no longer hold a grooming brush, or tighten a girth, or even mount my beloved mare without leading her into the gully by our pasture fence, I saw the writing on the stable wall and found a good home for her.

After selling my first story, I was spurred on to submit to other horse publications. "Pumped," I believe, is the term in modern lingo. Before I knew what was happening, I was out of the starting gate and running in a field of fellow equine writers. While my old friends were playing cards at the senior center and enjoying bus trips and cruises, I was beginning a new career—at the ripe old age of sixty-six.

Writing for horse publications filled the equine-void in my life. I found material in the coolest places: breeding farms, training facilities, and at world-class horse shows and small country venues. I made two *and* four-legged friends at the Baltimore City Mounted Police stables, as well as polo matches, show barns, and racing stables. While I was cozying up with horsemen and taking copious notes, my husband was never far away—more often than not glued to his current "good read."

Even more rewarding than seeing my work in print was the enthusiastic response from readers. John and I were at a funeral home viewing one afternoon when I walked into the lounge where a young girl, possibly ten, was engrossed in a magazine. I perked up when I saw her riding boots and britches, then when I took a closer look at her reading material, my heart raced. It was *Young Rider*, a magazine that ran my stories. I recognized the cover of the current edition—the one I had received in the mail that very day.

"That must be a pretty interesting magazine," I said. (I'm not beyond a shameless fishing expedition.)

She glanced briefly at the boring old lady before returning to the magazine. "Uh-huh."

"So...does it have stories, or just articles?"

"Oh, there's always a story. That's my favorite part. I read it first."

There was more, but who can remember? I didn't tell her I had written that story or that it was based on a true news story that had taken place near our son's neighborhood in South Florida. Why destroy any illusions she might have about the author wearing a riding outfit and sitting astride her horse with a laptop?

I had written it after reading an article in the *Florida Horsemen Magazine* about a Belgian draft horse named Duke, who had helped clean up his neighborhood after Hurricane Wilma. It was titled "Heroic Horse Helps Haul After Hurricane Wilma." I've always had a soft spot for draft horses; my beloved old Jet had Percheron in his pedigree. So, voilà! And I couldn't resist using the names of my granddaughters' two little dogs, Jasper and Lucky. This is the short story that was being enjoyed by the young horse enthusiast.

"Neighborhood Heroes"
Young Rider, Jan/Feb 2008

Sometimes Beth told people she had two brothers, but strictly speaking, that wasn't true. Jasper and Lucky might seem like part of the family, but they were still horses. The powerful Belgians worked in the family's carriage business. Tourists loved nothing better than sightseeing from a horse-drawn carriage, and they were willing to pay generously for the privilege.

At home, sometimes Beth climbed onto Jasper's or Lucky's broad back and joined her neighbor, Kathy, for a ride through the cool woods.

"Kathy's always bragging about the ribbons her thoroughbreds win," Beth told her parents. "Their pictures have even been in the newspapers." She'd never mentioned to Kathy that Jasper and Lucky had pulled plows at their previous home. "Carriage horses" sounded more refined than "workhorses."

The two carriages went out every day during decent weather. And in southern Florida, thanks to mild ocean breezes and tropical sun, the weather was almost always perfect—except during hurricane season.

Beth worked alongside her parents, harnessing the gentle Belgians and hitching them to the six-passenger carriages. That usually meant standing on a bench for the fourteen-year-old. Sometimes she even got to drive the carriages to their spot in the park, but there she had to turn over the reins to her father or mother.

"Tourists won't trust a fourteen-year-old girl to handle a big draft horse. If they don't feel safe, it will hurt business," her father said.

"But Dad, they're easy to drive. Besides, they know the route by heart." It was true. The horses knew where to turn, where to pause, and what to do when the only traffic light was red.

But her father was firm. "You can drive them when you're sixteen, not before."

Jasper and Lucky worked from sunup to sundown. Beth made sure there was always fresh water at their shady parking spot. While her parents slipped home for lunch, she removed the horses' bridles and fed them a midday meal of grain. When the bugs were bad, she wiped them with fly repellent.

It was mid-October when forecasters first mentioned a weather disturbance in the Caribbean. Tourists headed north when the hurricane warning was issued.

"We'd better get the horses home," said Beth's dad, even though the sun was still shining and the sky was blue. "We have a lot to do."

Beth knew the drill by heart. Anything that could blow away was brought inside. Shutters were placed over the house windows, and the barn windows were covered with plywood. Beth gave the horses extra hay and water. By the time they were bedded down in their sturdy, cinder block barn, the wind had blown in from the south, and threatening dark clouds swirled above.

There would be little sleep that night. Howling winds roared like jetfighters overhead, as a driving rain pelted the house hour after hour. Beth and her parents were huddled in the laundry room with emergency supplies when a loud crash caused Beth to leap from her chair.

"The horses!" she cried, hugging her mother.

"They're fine," said Mom. "That barn is a fortress."

"I couldn't see anything outside," Dad said minutes later. "There's probably a tree down."

The battery-powered radio warned people to stay put as the eye of the hurricane passed. By early morning, the wind had subsided, and the rain slowed to a drizzle.

Destruction was widespread, and emergency rescue crews could not meet the great demand.

Beth and her parents were relieved to find that their small farm had weathered the storm with minimal damage. While Beth checked the horses, her dad and mom checked on the neighbors.

"Beth! Beth! Help!"

Beth rushed from the barn to see Kathy running frantically across the wet driveway, dodging limbs and piles of debris.

"A tree crashed through our stable roof last night, and another one fell across the front. We can't reach the horses, and I know they're hurt." She began sobbing. "We called 911, and nobody can help us."

"Get my father," said Beth, pointing to a neighbor's house across the road. As Kathy hurried toward the road, Beth went into action. Ten minutes later, when Dad and Kathy ran through the yard, Lucky was harnessed and ready to go.

"Smart thinking," Dad said as Kathy's father joined them in the drive. "I'll get some rope to put around the trees. Maybe Lucky can pull them away from the stable."

"Oh, I don't know," said Kathy's dad, shaking his head. "Dragging heavy trees is not the same as pulling a carriage on wheels."

"He can do it," Beth insisted as they made their way to the damaged barn. "He used to pull a plow on a farm," she said proudly. She patted the horse's shoulder while the men attached the rope to the back of the harness, then to the fallen tree.

"Gidd-up, Lucky!" yelled Beth, holding the reins.

Lucky lowered his head and leaned into the harness. Beth didn't know whether to cheer or cry as his powerful shoulders and haunches strained against the weight. Finally, the heavy tree began to move ever so slightly at first, then was gradually pulled away from the stable.

While Kathy and her father rescued the horses from the collapsing building, Lucky, Beth, and Dad dragged the heavy tree to the end of the pasture. Then they dragged two more trees from the driveway, adding them to the pile. Lucky didn't seem to notice the loud cracking and snapping of the branches. An hour later Jasper took over, pulling parts of neighbors' roofs and sheds from the street.

A veterinarian treated the Thoroughbreds' bleeding wounds, saying that the quick action had saved their lives. That evening, Kathy visited the two Belgians with apples and carrots and her camera. "You are super horses! You know that?" she said, hugging their powerful necks.

Two days later, the local paper showed a picture of Lucky and Jasper. The caption read: *Neighborhood Heroes*.

The day the carriage business resumed, Beth handed the reins to her dad at the park as usual, but he shook his head and folded his arms.

"You've proven you can handle horses."

Beth smiled as she held Lucky's reins. Not everybody had the privilege of working with "*real live heroes*."

<< • >>

Over the next decade, while continuing to dream of writing a book, I wrote constantly and published more than fifty of my stories and articles not only in horse publications but in newspapers and mainstream magazines. Shelves that once held folders bulging with rejection letters now held notebooks bulging with newspaper and magazine clippings of my articles and essays—indeed, entire magazines with my stories.

Stories about loved ones continue to be especially meaningful. Many of them were written for holidays. What fun remembering my grandmother in the following true Labor Day story.

"Those Lazy Days of Yore, Before Women Started Working"
The Baltimore Sun, Labor Day, 2013

I was in the doctor's waiting room when I overheard a jaw-dropping conversation between some young women.

"I've been too busy to take my break," complained a receptionist sitting at a computer and sipping from a Starbuck's cup.

"Thank God it's Friday!" said another young woman carrying a stack of folders.

A third, who had been scheduling appointments, put down the receiver and said, "The weekend can't get here fast enough for me. I'm just going to veg out."

Then came the part that made my jaw drop.

"I really envy my grandmother and my great-grandmother. Can you imagine not having to work? They got to stay at home all day while their husbands supported the family."

"Yeah," said the one who was looking forward to the weekend. "The good old days. Those women really knew what leisure time was!"

According to the National Bureau of Labor Statistics, women did not begin "working" in earnest until the mid-twentieth century. Can you believe that?

Apparently, the only labor my grandmother experienced in the early 1900s was in the front bedroom, where she gave birth to six children—and slept her way to the top rung of the domestic ladder. The hussy!

Grandma Daisy was one of those lucky women who didn't have to work. While her husband was away on a commercial fish boat earning a living, she lollygagged around the homestead enjoying her brood. Thank God she had the occasional chore to save her from a life of endless tedium.

By the time those girls behind the desk arrived at work in the morning, Daisy had already gathered hens' eggs for breakfast, lopped the head off a rooster, and raked chicken manure for her garden. Then the leisure began in earnest as she pulled on her high rubber boots and made her way to the backyard vegetable patch.

She threw down her hoe from time to time and ran into the house to investigate screaming, extinguish fires, or wrestle sharp scissors from toddlers. Then it was back to hoeing weeds, dispatching poisonous snakes, and picking tomatoes. On wash day, she pumped water from the well, heated it, scrubbed clothes in a metal washtub beneath the apple tree, and then pegged them out on rope stretched across the lawn.

Hauling water from the well, wood from the shed, and slop buckets to the outhouse weren't really work. After all, it wasn't as though she was being paid. She was merely filling the empty hours until women could officially begin "working."

There was no glass ceiling in the world of Daisy's daily domestic drudgery. She had risen immediately to the pinnacle of her domain.

I couldn't help wondering how my grandmother might have responded to the young women at the desks. She might have agreed with them. Hers was, in fact, a labor of love. Daisy had been right where she wanted to be. Even if there were no pension checks or gold watches or golden parachutes at the end of her working years, there were six grateful, productive children who shared a common goal—to give their hardworking, widowed mother a well-deserved and peaceful retirement.

And to think, I had considered myself a working woman—albeit one who came home to a dishwasher, a microwave oven, a washing machine, and a dryer. Silly me!

Happy Labor Day. Next time you feel like you're working too hard, think about your great-grandmother.

After this story was printed, I received an email from a reader. Though I can't recall her name, the essence of her message is etched in my mind.

"I love your writing, Mrs. Rowe. Your stories make me feel good. I cut them out and save them in a scrapbook I call, My Happy Book. Whenever I'm feeling sad, I take it out and read one of your stories and feel better. Thank you, Mrs. Rowe. Please, keep on writing."

≪ • ≫

There is no better way to relive memorable relationships than through writing. Like much of my other work, the following Mother's Day story was written well before it was published. I had my own children in mind at the time and made sure they all received a copy.

"All Your Mother Wants Today Is You"
The Baltimore Sun, May 13, 2018

A recent national survey concluded that the most popular Mother's Day gifts are flowers, apparel, and gift cards. Ha! How could we get it so wrong?

I'm reminded of one woman's response when she was asked if she knew when Mother's Day was: "Mother's Day is any day my children call me."

There's only one thing your mother wants on Mother's Day—and that's you! Talk to her! I speak as the mother of three sons who, for years, communicated only when it was necessary:

You need to sign this permission slip, Mom."

"I'm in the concert choir, Mom. I need a tux."

"I need the car Saturday night."

"Can we have pizza tonight?"

Set aside an hour and call her, especially if she's a senior like me whose sons have moved as far away as they can get and still live in the USA. When you call, ask about her arthritis, and cover the receiver when you yawn.

Let her complain about unreasonable Aunt Grace—and take her side, even if you know Aunt Grace is right.

Ask how her mah-jongg game is and turn the page of your morning paper quietly as she tells you in excruciating detail.

Tell her something about your job and your friends. Above all, don't be in a hurry—not today. You have a lot to atone for. Look at all those years your poor mother had to impersonate Perry Mason to learn what was going on in your life. When you won a music award in middle school, she had to hear about it on the streets. And when you got the highest SAT score in high school, she had to learn about it at your graduation. And imagine your mother having to hide her surprise in choir the Sunday morning her fellow alto said, "Did you ever think that our children would be dating each other? And it looks serious."

Celebrating Mother's Day is easier if your mother lives nearby. Does she have a car? Wash it. Does she have a garden? Weed it. Does she attend religious services? Go with her; let her show you off. Better still, arrange with your workplace for a Take-Your-Mom-to-Work Day. Unless, of course, you're a crab fisherman on the Bering Sea or a test pilot or a gynecologist. Then you should probably stick with a bouquet of daisies and a box of Whitman's cream-centers.

The closest I ever came to taking my mother to work with me was when she stopped by our house in the morning on her way to the office. Typically, the front door would open, and she would observe me hard at work doing my job—reading to three little boys on the sofa, all of us still in pajamas. After her typical greeting, —"My, it must be nice to have all your housework done," she tore through the downstairs like a minesweeper, picking up a puzzle here and a stuffed animal there, tucking toy trucks and cowboy boots under her arms on her way to the playroom. As she deposited the toys, she could be heard mumbling, "There, now that wasn't so hard, was it?" Minutes later she kissed her three grandsons and disappeared, prompting astute observations such as, "What's housework, Mommy?"

Celebrating my mom on Mother's Day back then was easy: an invitation to a neat, orderly house with three clean grandsons, an attentive husband, and a well-cooked meal. Once a year it didn't kill me, and it won't kill you either. I promise.

≪ ◆ ≫

It's never too late to honor a loved one through writing. This brief Father's Day tribute in memory of my dad remains one of my all-time favorite published short pieces.

"The Best Gift Dad Ever Got"
The Baltimore Sun, June 19, 2019—Father's Day

There was nothing complicated about Father's Day in my family. My mother bought my father a gift, and I presented it to him. Something practical for a hard-working man: a shirt, a modest tie for Sundays, some big white handkerchiefs. Dad was never without a big white handkerchief.

Never French cologne. Or Italian loafers. Or gold cuff links. Uh-uh! Not for my father. And God forbid he should open a box and find a gold chain necklace or bracelet. The only jewelry my father ever wore was a watch with a leather band.

When I was old enough to shop, Old Spice was my standby. Dad always acted surprised, even though the shape of the bottle was a dead giveaway. To this day, the familiar smell of Old Spice reminds me of my father.

One year I gave him chocolate-covered cherries, his favorite. He took one and passed the box around the room. It came back empty. The next time I gave him two boxes of chocolate-covered cherries.

Dad was happiest when he was making someone else happy. I was fifteen when he converted an old chicken house into a first-rate stable and fenced in a pasture so that his obsessed daughter could have a horse. The first time I rode my horse in a show was on Father's Day 1954. Dad bought a hitch, attached it to his work truck, and we borrowed a dilapidated wooden horse trailer from an old friend. While my father rebuilt the rotted floor and repaired the sagging tailgate, I scrubbed manure stains from my horse's gray coat and shined his hooves.

I won a yellow ribbon that day, my very first, for a third-place finish in a class of a dozen horses. Afterward, I handed the ribbon to Dad and said, "Happy Father's Day." He told me it was his favorite gift ever! I still have that ribbon, and I expect I always will. It's in a box stuffed with horse show ribbons—on the top, wrapped in a big white handkerchief.

Chapter 8

IN MY HEAD

JOHN AND I WERE GUESTS AT A WEDDING THAT WAS more highly produced than a movie. The bride was a friend's granddaughter we barely knew, and the groom had been touted as a brilliant young certified public accountant; he looked to be about sixteen. The affair took place in a community hall where the photographers and videographers outnumbered the wedding party. Or at least, I think they did. It's hard to be certain, as camera tripods obscured our view of the ceremony.

"Why are we here?" my husband whispered. "I don't know these people. I feel like an extra on a movie set." I apologized again and explained that I couldn't get out of it. "The dinner will be good!" I promised. When the couple kissed, I expected somebody to clap one of those slate boards together and yell, "Take one!" That was a mere overture to the main event.

At the reception, the wedding party burst through the doors performing choreographed dance routines. I couldn't take my eyes off the young groom as he cartwheeled across the floor to the head table like a Cirque du Soleil performer.

I must have stared off because John looked me square in the eye and asked, "Okay, where are you now, Maggie?"

My husband knows when I'm "in my head," as he calls it—when I've seen or heard something that sends my mind on a freewheeling excursion through time to some long-forgotten character or event. It can happen anywhere . . . even at a wedding reception. I couldn't wait to get home to my computer to tell the story of another CPA who had cartwheeled his way through my childhood—in quite a different manner. As with much of my writing, the story of Mr. Brann has not been shared . . . until now.

"A Touch of Class"

Who knows why some characters cross our paths barely noticed while others leave an indelible impression? Perhaps they come into our lives during a more sensitive time when we have a heightened awareness. Perhaps they're out of the ordinary.

Mr. Brann was one of those people. Seventy years later, I can still see him clearly.

I was a child when my parents engaged the services of Mr. Brann. To me, he was "Mr. Sunday," always dressed like my father when he was on his way to church. That's how certified public accountants dressed back in the 1940s—just to sit at the dining room table and "reconcile the books." This particular CPA graced our home twice a year. And, boy, do I mean *graced*.

One day when my mother and I were looking through the Montgomery Ward catalog, I pointed and yelled, "Look! It's Mr. Sunday!" It was a picture of a distinguished man with a sprinkling of gray hair, wearing a business suit and carrying a small brown leather suitcase like the one Mr. Brann carried.

The first time I met him, I asked if he had brought his lunch, the way my big sister carried her lunch to school every day. He opened it and showed me. It smelled like my father's new shoes, and there was no food, just some papers and pens.

Typically, Dad would hang around to greet Mr. Brann in the morning before leaving for "the job" in his freshly laundered khakis and neatly ironed work shirt—before he had a chance to get his fingernails dirty.

I could always tell when Mr. Brann was coming—or Paul, as my parents called him. There were telltale signs. Our house was usually spotless, but on those days, I could see my face reflected in the dining room table. That's where he would pore over Mom's books—with her beside him to answer questions. The morning sun reflecting off the silver service on the buffet was enough to burn your retinas. I'd learned that phrase from a story in my sister's *Weekly Reader* about people in some foreign country who go blind from staring at the sun.

If all this wasn't enough, my mother's outfit was a dead giveaway. She'd show up in the kitchen that morning in a pretty dress—on a weekday! *When she wasn't even going out*. A hint of Chanel N° 5 followed her everywhere— kind of like the sickening stench that followed our dog around after he rolled in something dead. Chanel N° 5 was Mom's scent of choice when she and Dad went out with their hoity-toity Lions Club friends.

My mother was the bookkeeper for my father's electrical contracting business, and she knew from the get-go that there was more to Mr. Brann than his auditing skills. I could tell by the way she crossed her legs while they were working—lifting her toes high in the air and waving them about, like she did before standing up to address the women's auxiliary at church.

Oh yeah, this man was straight from a catalogue and brought a touch of class to our modest home on Leslie Avenue. He was not the sort of man Mom would have run into in the small fishing village where she was raised. He was more like the men she might run into in the books she devoured—men of refinement and culture.

I had my own reasons for looking forward to Mr. Sunday's visits—although I wasn't allowed to call him Mr. Sunday or Mr. Catalogue or even Paul. That wouldn't be proper. And when it came to *proper* behavior, my mother had high standards.

I made it a point to leave my backyard virtual-pony and come into the house midmorning when Mr. Brann and Mom were settled at the dining room table with the books in front of them—and maybe a serving of fresh apple strudel and a cup of coffee. Mr. Brann had confessed on his first visit that apple strudel was his weakness, so naturally it was ready and waiting on the days he was expected.

Whenever I came through the door, our CPA would rise from his chair and bow toward me as though a beautiful princess had entered the room—instead of a kid wearing cowboy boots and a Dale Evans fringed skirt. I was careful not to shoot off my cap pistol in the house, lest my mother's eyebrows shoot upward in disapproval. That would be a perfect example of *im*proper behavior.

"Well, hello there, young lady," he'd say with delight, as though he'd been waiting for me all morning and now his life was complete. "And how are we today?"

He always smelled like Daddy when he and Mom were going to a Lions Club affair. On one visit, Mr. Sunday smiled at me, opened his brown suitcase, and reached inside. It reminded me of the way a magician I saw at the carnival reach into a big black hat. Only instead of pulling out a white rabbit, Mr. Brann pulled out a horse figurine, which he presented to me with a little bow. "A token of my regard, Miss Peggy."

It made me giggle when he talked like that—and Mom too. Surely, there was nobody more proper than Mr. Brann. A gentleman to the core. I think even Emily Post—the etiquette authority my mother was forever quoting—would have been impressed by our Mr. Brann.

I was a teenager by the time we moved to the farm, where there was plenty of room for Dad's expanding business, as well as my *real* horses.

Now when Mr. Brann came to audit our books, he and Mom worked in our basement office. Thanks to my father's construction skills, it was state of the art 1954, with wood-paneled walls, linoleum flooring, and an acoustical tile ceiling, plus fluorescent lighting and a black telephone. Mom referred to it as the "terrace office," because it had an outside entrance from the driveway— but it was still in the basement, which I had once referred to as "the cellar." And, boy, I never did that again. Big mistake! Cellars were damp and filthy with dirt floors, apparently.

Except for the gray hair, which had spread considerably, our CPA's appearance never altered over the years, nor did his formality. He still set a high bar for refinement, that's for sure—dressing like Chet Huntley and David Brinkley on the evening news, and never speaking casually or using slang. If you'd seen him in public, you might have assumed he was one of those diplomats who knew how to speak French. Mom still treated him like royalty, and even after she found her calling in real estate, she cleared her schedule to spend the day with Paul when he came to audit the books.

I was returning from school one day as Mom was showing Mr. Brann to the door. I heard her tell him that our business was thriving just in time to support two big horses and my sister's college tuition.

I look back on Mr. Brann's fall from grace with bewilderment. I learned of it quite suddenly at dinner one evening, along with my father, who was equally shocked. It was on his second or third visit to our state-of-the-art basement office, after he and Mom had spent much of the day together working on the books.

It would be his final visit.

I was engrossed in my own life, but this was momentous. In retrospect, my mother had been quiet at dinner that evening—until Dad asked, "How did things go with Paul today, hon?" as he lifted a piece of succulent beef from his homemade vegetable soup and placed it in a saucer. He was shaking ketchup onto the beef when he stopped and looked up. "Is everything all right with the books?"

I was trying to imagine Mr. Brann shaking a ketchup bottle when it occurred to me that my mother wasn't answering Dad's question. A few seconds later she replied, "Mr. Brann behaved improperly today." She said it in the same way she might have said, "Peggy was suspended from school today." With a mixture of disappointment and disbelief.

Now my mother was not one for spreading malicious rumors or even speaking of unpleasantries. I had learned the "do not gossip" rule years earlier. It always ended with the same lecture: "If you can't say something nice about someone, don't say anything at all!" So naturally, her statement about Mr. Brann got my attention as well as my father's.

"Are there problems with the books?" Dad asked.

Mom put down her soup spoon, smoothed the napkin across her lap, and looked at Dad. "Paul asked me to go out with him today."

"What? You mean . . . on a *date*?" And then my father made a big mistake. He laughed. Like he'd just made the funniest joke ever.

"He invited me to go out to lunch with him! To a restaurant! Just the two of us! Alone."

And then Dad made his second big mistake of the day. "Oh, hon, he didn't mean anything improper. He just wants to repay you for all the coffee and strudel you've served him through the years. That's all. It was nothing personal! I'm sure of that." He smacked the bottom of the ketchup bottle, innocently, as Mom stiffened and set her jaw.

After staring for a few seconds, as if trying to decide if this was sound reasoning or the ultimate insult, she said in her outside voice, "It was inappropriate! I'm a married woman! He's a married man! It wouldn't be proper!"

And that was it. My mother said no more on the subject. She'd never been one to take me into her confidence—ever. So my teenage brain was left to speculate. And speculate it did.

I didn't mention the obvious—that if Mr. Brann had impure thoughts or even intentions, a secluded office would be the place to act on them, not a public restaurant.

Had Mr. Brann behaved more inappropriately than my mother let on? Had this paragon of refinement misread her attention to him through the years, lost his balance, and fallen from his perch on that pedestal of propriety? Causing my mother's "flight of fancy" to crash? Or had my mother hoped for something more from him—something a little more daring, perhaps? Was she secretly disappointed that he didn't make a pass at her? Of course, I could be overthinking it. She was, after all, of an advanced age—in her forties.

It was a cliff-hanger, to be sure. Like the soap operas Mom used to listen to on the radio—each episode leaving her suspended and wanting more.

I never saw Mr. Brann again, and my mother never spoke of him. He hadn't lived up to her Victorian standards of proper behavior. And that was that. Or so we were led to believe.

Years later when Mom disapproved of my boyfriend, whom I would go on to marry, I was tempted to say, "Well, he might not be as classy as Mr. Brann—but at least he didn't ask my mother for a date."

I refrained. Mom wasn't known for her sense of humor.

Chapter 9

MAKING A DIFFERENCE

IHAVE THE GREATEST RESPECT FOR REAL WORKING writers. I mean the ones who hustle to find a story, pitch it, conduct an interview, and write it. Like my friend and editor, Michele, who also writes articles for professional publications, national magazines, and websites. She considers herself a freelancer. But I, on the other hand, have never pitched a story or had an assignment—or even a deadline. I've written stories and articles on topics that have interested *me* and submitted some of them to various publications.

I'd love to say that my freelance writing salary has put food on the table and paid the mortgage. But it would be a lie. If John and I had depended on my income as a writer, we'd have eaten beans and lived in a crate. It was my husband's teaching salary and good sense when it came to finances that provided our family's security.

When it came to writing, the big payoff came in 2002 when I wrote a letter to the Baltimore Orioles's front office about their number one fan. A letter that resulted in an invitation for my ninety-year-old infirm mother to throw out an opening pitch at an Orioles game, which she would go on to describe as the most exciting experience of her life. Years later, I would write another such letter for my one-hundred-year-old friend, Mary, who received the same invitation. She, too, described it as the most exciting experience of her life.

Knowing that my writing has impacted someone else's life in a positive way is as good as it gets. Such was the case in 2012 when I wrote the following story about our neighbor, Chick Serio.

"For Gallantry in Action"
The Baltimore Sun, 2012—Memorial Day

In 2001, my husband and I moved from our home in "rural suburbia" to a retirement condo. The move was my idea, but John was a good sport about it—eventually. His main objection was the proximity of so many strangers.

"So much for privacy," he complained. "What if they're horrible people? Have you thought about that?"

Shortly after moving in, we met our new neighbors across the hall, Chick and Marguerite Serio—a friendly, older couple with grown children and grandkids. Just two average, normal people like John and me—or so we thought. We were mistaken.

I still remember that day John came barreling through the door, reminiscent of the kids rushing in after an adventure that simply had to be shared. He had news that would elevate Chick Serio's status from that of "nice old neighbor" to "superhero."

"Guess what, hon! Marguerite told me that Chick was awarded the Silver Star for gallantry in action on Iwo Jima!" John said. *"We're living across the hall from a genuine war hero!"*

You would never have guessed that Chick Serio was a war hero to look at him. He didn't wear an Iwo Jima baseball cap, or a Marine Corps jacket, or have a Semper Fi flag hanging from his balcony. A modest man, he didn't even display his Silver Star medal. In fact, when John asked to see it, Chick wasn't sure exactly where it was. "Somewhere in the house. Marguerite would know," he said.

Chick was an ordinary Baltimorean in many ways—with a passion for his family, his church, and his country. To top it off, he had an appetite for steamed crabs and a sixty-year-long love affair with the Baltimore Orioles.

Yet he had answered his country's call more than seventy years ago.

This was the beginning of a special relationship for John. Not just because my husband was a history buff and had taught the subject or because he had served in Korea. But because John has a fascination with World War II and an entire generation of heroes who are slipping away.

Chick had a story and, as a writer, I needed to hear it—and tell it. However, we soon learned that our friend was hesitant to talk about his life in the military. It was years before I broached the subject and asked if he would be willing to share some of his stories with me. Finally, to my surprise and delight, our neighbor, now in his nineties, agreed.

So one spring afternoon I walked across the hall with a yellow legal pad, a pencil, and a camera. For the next couple of hours, I sat across the room from Chick while he talked about *his* war. I could see Marguerite around the corner at the kitchen table with a cup of coffee and the morning paper. From time to time as Chick spoke, she rose silently and refilled her cup.

The first thing I learned that day was that Chick Serio was *not* a *hero*. About that, he was adamant.

"The heroes were the men and boys who did not come home or who returned disabled. Six thousand of them right here in Maryland!" he said.

I was expecting to hear a story about a young man with lofty ideals who was hell-bent on saving his country and preserving his family's freedom. Instead, I heard a story about an innocent, naïve, unpretentious young man who had grown up with his own personal hero and best friend—his Uncle Joe Marsiglia—just a year or two his senior. Chick was twenty when Joe received his notice from the draft board in 1942, and Chick was determined not to be left behind. With visions of fighting beside his buddy, he decided to enlist.

When Chick's father, John Serio, saw how determined his son was, he relented and made one stipulation: "Join the Navy, son! You'll have a clean bed on a ship instead of sleeping in a filthy hole in the ground."

But when the two young men arrived at the armory, there was a long line at the Navy recruitment office.

At this point, Chick looked at me with a boyish grin and shrugged. "We figured the Marines needed men more than the Navy did, so Joe and I both signed up. When I told my father...man, I'd never seen him so furious."

Our friend reflected on boot camp at Parris Island where he was told that "a Marine can do anything!"

"And I believed it," he said. He spoke warmly of his schooling and training at Camp Lejeune, and in time, his promotion to sergeant—almost as though he were at a school reunion reliving fond memories of old friends and daring escapades.

Then came the final, intense training on the beaches of beautiful Hawaii where they practiced assault landings and had time to play some baseball.

Chick paused in his story, and I feared that the dreaded next chapter would not be shared—at least that day. But after a short walk, he returned and continued.

Interestingly, at this point in the story, Chick speaks of his war experience in the present, as though he's reliving it instead of just telling a story. And it feels like I'm there beside him on that long, unforgettable journey in the crowded, dark hold of a ship—surrounded by an unbearable, nauseating stench of body odor and vomit.

It's on the deck of that very ship that Sgt. Serio first hears the words *Iwo Jima* and learns of its strategic importance in the planned invasion of Japan.

"It's February 19, 1945," Chick recalls, "and we're watching from the safety of our ship in horror as the first wave of Marines makes their landing onto the island. We see American boys flying through the air and falling onto the sand. Enemy mortars are exploding everywhere."

Chick shakes his head, and I worry that the memory is too real. But he continues. "We keep watching and waiting—helpless. Night comes, and we sleep. The next morning, we can't believe our breakfast—steak and eggs! We no sooner finish when they tell us to pack up our gear; it's our turn."

He goes on to describe "enormous swells in a white sea and the hazardous rope ladders down the side of the ship," and shakes his head in disbelief. "Some guys—*boys*—never even make it to the beach; they fall into the deep, dark water between the ship and the landing boat and drown before they can be rescued. Others break their legs and are put back on the ship. Chick shakes his head sadly and looks at me. "They didn't even have a chance to fight."

I glance into the kitchen and realize that Marguerite, no longer turning the pages of her paper, is staring out the window, her coffee forgotten.

"When the boats reach land, the flaps are lowered, and the seasick Marines of the Fifth Pioneer Battalion, Fifth Marine Division join men from other landing craft running onto the black volcanic sand, littered with debris ... and Marines, dead and alive."

I couldn't help but react at this point in his story. "Oh, Chick," I said, "how does a person live with such memories?"

He told me that sixty-seven years later, he still awakens from nightmares and relives the terror of life in a succession of foxholes. He spoke of Japanese soldiers emerging from caves, running toward him screaming, brandishing guns and bayonets, being ready to die, watching a buddy standing up beside him and being shot dead, shooting his gun blindly, and knowing he killed men without feeling remorse. He spent four days of intense fighting with no chance to even remove his boots or go to the latrine. He used his helmet to soak his sore feet—then as a toilet.

Chick spoke of lulls in the fighting; spending quiet moments to reflect on a house in Walbrook, Maryland; taking time to remember the bustling produce stall at Lexington Market that had supported three generations of Serios; time to remember his very first job at the age of eight...selling grocery bags to shoppers; time to remember Mount Saint Joe High School and his Italian father's advice about enlisting—and knowing that he had been right. There was time to ache for family, and most of all, moments to mourn his Uncle Joe, whom he had not seen since basic training, and who lay critically wounded in a hospital.

Then came that fateful day on March 26 when his unit was under fierce attack and running out of ammunition. Acting on impulse, Sgt. Serio commandeered a jeep and drove through enemy fire to the ammo dump on the beach—shooting four enemy soldiers along the way. At the dump, a sergeant and the major in command refused his request for more ammo.

In desperation, Chick leveled his rifle at their heads and yelled, "Men are dying while we're talking." The major and sergeant backed down, and Chick's men loaded the jeep with ammunition.

He later learned that, as a result of his actions that day, a US assault team was able to successfully counter the Japanese attack. Sgt. Charles A. Serio received the Silver Star for valor in recognition of his resourcefulness in the closing battle for Iwo Jima.

As I left the Serio house that day following my interview, Marguerite followed me into the hall and told me something that was hard to believe.

"Peggy, Chick has never ever talked about his war experience—in seventy years!" she said, shaking her head. "I have never heard these stories before today. I just figured he'd moved on and forgotten them. He was busy earning a law degree, then starting his own insurance agency, and supporting a family of six. Anyway, thank you, thank you, Peggy, for giving me a chance to finally know what it was like. I can't wait to read your story!"

<< • >>

When the story was published, my email address was included at the end in keeping with the *Sun*'s policy. As a result, the following day my inbox was flooded with messages—some were for me but the majority of them were for Chick—filled with praise and gratitude for his service. Some were from strangers. Others were from relatives, friends, and colleagues.

The Serios, like many of their generation, were not up on computer technology in 2012. So John and I invited them to our condo that Memorial Day afternoon for lunch. Chick wore his Marine uniform for the occasion. He was surprised that almost all of the buttons could fasten.

After lunch, John brought his laptop to the dining room table, and for well over the next hour, Chick and Marguerite sat transfixed with glistening eyes as he read dozens of emails from admirers, as well as old friends.

Chick spoke of his strong faith in the Lord that brought him through the turmoil of war and its aftermath. He expressed how fortunate he felt to have lived to see the National World War II Memorial in Washington, D.C., and to witness the resurgence of interest in all things World War II, especially movies and best-selling books.

Most of all, Chick was grateful that his Uncle Joe had survived his serious injuries and returned home to a full life, despite being terribly disfigured by enemy fire.

As they left our house, Chick hugged me and said, "Thank you! This has been the best Memorial Day of my life!" There were actual tears all around. Like many other ninety-three-year-old men, our friend and neighbor was feeble and bent. And still, we looked up to him.

I was grateful for two things that day: the greatest generation who fought the good fight so that others could live peacefully and the privilege of making a difference in the life of one so deserving.

Chapter 10

THE SHORTER AND THE PLAINER, THE BETTER

I'M NOT KNOWN FOR LONG, COMPLEX SENTENCES LIKE Charles Dickens or William Faulkner wrote. Not that I would presume to compare my work to theirs. Not by a long shot.

In general, I follow the advice of Beatrix Potter: "The shorter and the plainer, the better." And Mark Twain who said: "As to the adjective ... when in doubt, wipe it out." My literary references are more likely to come from *Winnie the Pooh* than from Homer.

The following true story was a joy to write. Simple and straightforward, it is a reminiscence with my favorite and most beloved characters. I think that Mark Twain and Beatrix Potter would find it acceptable. I know that my children will. It has lived only on my computer ... until now.

"A Gentleman of Note"

It was 1972 when the old man stood in our living room peeling off layers of clothing the way one might peel layers from an onion: hat, glove, another glove, overcoat, scarf, sweater, vest ... and all of it smelling of woodsmoke.

Our three sons stared as if Mr. Kirk were a magician hired to entertain at a birthday party—juggling bowling pins in the air or pulling colored scarves from his pockets. He was probably the oldest man the children had ever met. And possibly the shortest, as ten-year-old Michael was a good three inches taller. As they watched, mesmerized, they sniffed the air, which was oddly reminiscent of a smoldering campfire. We would learn that Mr. Kirk heated his house with a woodstove, and we came to associate him with that aura. Even in the summer, his clothing seemed to exhale the odors of smoke and creosote.

"All right," I said, breaking their trance as the strip-tease ended. "You boys can get started on your homework now. I'll call you when it's time for your lesson. Phil, you'll be first, right after me. So don't go far."

On his way from the room, seven-year-old Scott put his head back, inhaled deeply, and said, "We haven't roasted marshmallows in a long time, Mom. Can we build a fire tonight?"

This musician had come highly recommended by a friend whose children were taking piano lessons. My half hour of instruction was always first so that I could start dinner while the others took their turns on the bench. My husband's lesson was last; he promised to get home from work in time. You'd have thought I had asked him to sit in on the lady's sewing circle instead of on a piano bench for half an hour once a week.

"You'll be setting a good example for the boys," I told him. "You know—a guy thing." Not that there wasn't some eye-rolling, but in the end, John agreed. Especially since Mr. Kirk charged a measly dollar fifty per lesson. Anyone else would have charged three times as much. But then, they wouldn't be in their upper eighties.

So Thursday afternoons I drove the five miles to pick up our teacher, and for the next two and one-half hours, our family took turns sitting beside him and playing the pieces we had practiced. The seven dollars and fifty cents was well within our budget, and it took no more effort to prepare dinner for six than it did for five. Although I always fixed something special—including a homemade dessert. Mr. Kirk was a bachelor.

I wasn't new to piano lessons. I've had a love/hate relationship with the instrument for as long as I can remember. In my first book, *About My Mother,* I describe in great detail how my unreasonable mother forced me to take lessons. She had dreams of her daughters playing at church functions and was in seventh heaven the Sunday my older sister filled in for the organist. For six years, I trudged to the Elmwood Piano Studio every Tuesday afternoon and humiliated myself for an interminable half hour.

Though she seemed an ancient relic at the time, my teacher was probably in her thirties or forties. Patient and motherly, she sensed from the get-go that I was hopeless when it came to the piano. I avoided practicing with the same intensity I avoided the neighborhood bully—and she could tell.

Each time I begged to quit the lessons, Mom's default response went into overdrive: "Piano lessons will give you an appreciation for music, Peggy. Some day you'll thank me ... blah, blah, blah, blah, blah ...." She repeated it so often, I heard it in my sleep. Getting on my mother's good side was as simple as learning to play an easy selection from our church hymnal. Nothing put Mom in a good mood like a good old-fashioned hymn. I might have lacked technique, but I played with feeling—*resentment!*

Mothers are smart. Years later, her prophecy would be fulfilled when John bought me the brand-new Kimball piano that now resided in our dining room by the stairway. Our three sons stabbed at the keys from time to time and became proficient at "Chopsticks," while I played Christmas carols and simplified arrangements of classical music. Nowadays, they can probably be found in a book titled *The Classics for Dummies.* My performances were peppered with mistakes, which made me regret squandering the years of lessons, as well as my parents' money, which I had argued at the time would have been better spent on a pony.

And now I had an opportunity to make up for those lost years. My weeks revolved around Thursdays. I spent every spare minute practicing—until even the dog shook her head and trotted from the room.

I was never far away during the children's lessons, stepping around the corner with a mixing bowl in my hands or a tea towel over my shoulder to listen to the clipped conversations or a short passage tentatively played by young fingers. Like my mother before me, I dreamed of my sons one day playing Beethoven.

Mr. Kirk was patient, pleasant, and perceptive. Speaking slowly in a deep, gravelly voice, and without a trace of frustration, he said to seven-year-old Scott, "Just ten more minutes, young man, and then you can get on with your homework."

To which Scott replied, "Oh, I finished my homework. I'm building a dam at the stream. Poppie built one there when he was my age—then he went swimming." Clever Mr. Kirk turned a few pages in the book and chose a simple tune for Scott's next assignment. He played it as Scott listened. It was called "The Babbling Brook," and I never once had to remind my son to practice it.

My favorite part of each lesson came at the end when our teacher moved from his chair to the bench and introduced our new assignments—playing them flawlessly. It was like a mini recital. Mr. Kirk was nearly as entertaining at the dinner table as he was at the piano. Week after week he regaled us with stories of growing up on a dairy farm—milking cows, cleaning the barn, and pouring pure cream over his morning cereal.

"Today they say that cream is bad for you, but it didn't seem to hurt me," said this octogenarian who still enjoyed excellent hearing and vision.

His stories were fascinating the first few times we heard them, but there were only so many stories, and eventually, we knew them by heart and could have finished any one of them after hearing the first sentence. The gratification I had hoped for in my children's musical accomplishments was never realized. But their kindness week after week—as they listened patiently to our old teacher's stories, pretending they were hearing them for the first time—was a source of pride.

My husband's lessons lasted only one month, as he claimed his fingers were not made for the keyboard. Mr. Kirk was understanding and not surprised.

"Adult fingers are not as flexible as children's," he told John. "Especially when they haven't played the piano as youngsters." John coped bravely with his disappointment.

Eventually I was the only Rowe who looked forward to the lessons and who practiced faithfully. That said, our children benefitted immeasurably from Mr. Kirk's tutelage. I like to think he gave our youngest a better understanding of history. I came close to dropping my favorite platter the day I stepped into the dining room where Phil's legs were swinging freely beneath the piano bench as he asked nonchalantly, "Did you know Jesus, Mr. Kirk?"

The old teacher smiled and said, "Oh, no. Jesus lived a long time before I was born, son. But I did hear Rachmaninoff play the piano in person many years ago." If our kindergartener was impressed, he kept it to himself.

During one lesson, he said to Mike, "You have an extraordinary ear, young man." That statement, once he realized the meaning, gave our shy ten-year-old the confidence to participate in school music programs. Of course, Mike would never be as gifted as Mr. Kirk, who

A local book event

Katie and Grandmom

Young Katie and Jessie Rowe

Phil, Mike, and Scott, who helped their
mom to see the humor in life

Peggy—after surgery for a suspicious red streak . . .

Elizabeth and Donna—Peggy's writing friends who
encouraged her and gave her good advice

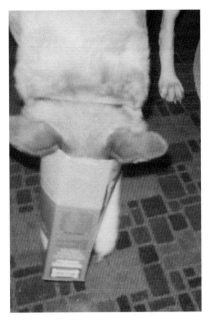

Shim, who foraged inside and out

Shim, a sweet dog with an odd concept of food

Thelma and her birthday cake

Thelma's colorful birthday cake

The dilapidated horse trailer Dad
rebuilt for Peggy's first horse show

Grandma Daisy—
lady of leisure

Mary Enlow, a friend who threw out the
opening pitch on her 100th birthday

Chick Serio—neighbor and war hero

Peggy, concert pianist—not

John and Peggy in NYC—with a celebrity look-alike

Old friends

More old friends

Peggy—holding her first book off the press

Peggy—recording her first audiobook

Peggy and Michele "Wojo" Wojciechowski,
first reader—holding their first books

The writers' room

The rubber duckies' adventures on Facebook

John—shooting his machine (Nerf) gun

Peggy—with John's new TV Ears, a life-changer

Peggy—practicing shooting the dreaded machine (Nerf) gun

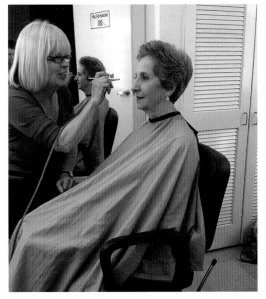

Dina getting Peggy ready for her TV close-up

John and Peggy on the first NYC book tour

Mike joins Peggy on a New Jersey book tour

Look what Peggy found!

Mike, Peg, and John—"This really is a terrific book, Mom!"

Peggy—in her writing room

had perfect pitch. The kids loved testing their teacher by having him close his eyes and identify the note they played. They could never fool him. Once, when Mr. Kirk was in the kitchen as Scott played a wrong note, he called out, "That's F natural, son."

I loved our teacher's sense of humor almost as much as his musical talent. When the doorbell chimed, he paused mid-sentence to say, "E-C. Major third." And one day during my lesson, before the children had returned from school, he got up to use the lavatory. He was about ten feet away when I heard him "toot." Without missing a beat, he said, as if to himself, "D flat, I think." We didn't speak of it, but both of us had smiles when he returned.

I was making progress with pieces such as "Moonlight Sonata" and Mozart's "Piano Sonata in C major" (but only the easy passages) and dreamed of accompanying our choir in the church sanctuary—or at least entertaining old friends at a party with a Scott Joplin medley.

The fact that I was nervous playing for Mr. Kirk was perplexing, but not surprising. I had a history of being nervous when playing in front of an audience—even family. I couldn't blame my teacher, as he was always positive and encouraging. The very same pieces I had played to perfection that morning were tentative and filled with errors as he sat beside me. Sometimes it was as though I had never seen the music before that moment.

"It's called *performance anxiety*," he explained, nodding sympathetically. "And it's not unusual, especially in adults who haven't performed before audiences as children."

One Thursday I sat at the piano before my lesson as Mr. Kirk used the nearby bathroom. While waiting, I played my two assigned pieces perfectly, as I had done on the preceding days.

"That was lovely!" my teacher said when he rejoined me. After making some suggestions concerning dynamics, he had me play the pieces again. I can only say that a stranger coming into the room would have assumed I had developed sudden-onset paralysis of the fingers. It was that bad. And discouraging. Alas, it did not improve, and it seemed my future in performance wasn't to be.

When the children's interest waned, I imagined my mother watching from her window with a smile on her face as I hunted them down like fugitives at lesson time screaming, "Piano lessons will give you an appreciation for music…You'll thank me some day!"

We took lessons until Mr. Kirk developed health issues. His passion for music and his very presence affected all of us, and I've never regretted our family's yearlong keyboard journey together. It did, indeed, contribute to my children's appreciation for music. I've been reminded of it frequently through the years. Like the day John and I shopped at Phil's secondhand bookstore to the accompaniment of Vivaldi's "Four Seasons" playing in the background. Or the day I climbed into Scott's pickup and the speakers blared Beethoven's "Minuet in G major."

"Oh, Scott," I said. "I always dreamed you would play Beethoven for me one day."

And who could forget that episode of *Dirty Jobs* where Mike cleaned a massive pipe organ in a Philadelphia church, then proceeded to play a few measures of a favorite classical piece—the only three measures he knew, most likely—but fans were impressed.

I occasionally play simple hymns for our church's evening events. The friendly group adjusts their expectations and continue singing when I lose my place. They chalk it up to nerves—and rightly so.

During the COVID-19 quarantine, church friends have been impressed by my Zoom accompaniments. I don't tell them my secret—that I practice endlessly—then prerecord the selections on my keyboard. When the time comes, I sit on the bench with the computer camera behind me, push the "Play" button, and move my hands over the keyboard with confidence. Not once do I land on the wrong key.

Somehow, I think Mr. Kirk would approve.

Chapter 11

A CRITIC INDEED

EVERY WRITER NEEDS A BRAVE CRITIC. SOMEONE who's not afraid to tell the truth. "Your ending is weak," or "Your plot is thin," or "It needs to be funnier." It's hard to imagine my journey without Mike—listening, laughing, and cheering me on. The fact that his very public career is also the source of endless, entertaining material has been the icing on my literary cake. The following story is a perfect example.

"Roadkill: The Dirty Parents"

My husband and I were watching *Dirty Jobs* reruns one Saturday when the "Roadkill Cleaner" episode came on. Instead of grimacing, as we normally would, we exchanged glances—the way people do when they share a naughty secret.

It was one of the earliest episodes, and like most viewers, John and I were sickened by the sheer volume of carcasses on highways. There was an upside, of course. As with most stories on *Dirty Jobs*, this episode reeked of educational opportunity. In fact, my husband had often claimed that viewing all three hundred episodes of *Dirty Jobs* is the equivalent of a three-credit college course.

As always, our son came away from this job with an appreciation for the workers who pick up an average of one thousand animals—mostly deer, opossums, and raccoons—from Ohio roadways in one year. Without this crew, highways would be impassable. Who knew? And through it all, their sensitivity toward animals remains intact. Mike demonstrated that it's a job requiring a strong back and an even stronger stomach.

Shortly after the episode aired, our son sent us a gift. Actually, he *forwarded a* gift to us that he had received in the mail. And no, it wasn't a carcass from the road—not exactly.

It wasn't Mike's first *Dirty Jobs* gift. We've saved some of them through the years—the ones that haven't drawn flies or grown mildew or rotted and stunk to high heaven. Like the little pots made of cow manure from a dairy farm in Connecticut; the little pellets of owl vomit wrapped in foil; and something from a goat—possibly cheese or soap. Of course, it could have been worse. We held our breath after he worked with worms and maggots and were afraid to go to our mailbox after he castrated sheep.

In contrast, we had high hopes when we saw our son in an opal mine—no such luck.

Anyway, his gift arrived in November—four identical place mats, sturdy and well-made, with a large photograph of what initially appeared to be a Rorschach inkblot. They were mostly red in color. But as we stared at it, two ears gradually emerged, then an eye came into focus and a leg. Oh yeah, it was a picture of roadkill all right—a rabbit in a former life. Perhaps one of the thousands of animals picked up from the stretch of road where he'd spent a day.

It was hideous and offensive, of course, and John said something like, "I guess we should be grateful it's not the real thing." I stuck the place mats in the bottom desk drawer along with my lovely Currier and Ives prints and put them out of my mind. What did our son expect me to do? Serve lunch on them to my old teacher friends? With an entree of rabbit cacciatore perhaps? Or a tasty bunny kebab?

But, of course, the worst was yet to come.

A humorist looks at the world around her and sees the humor—it comes naturally. The challenge is in revealing that humor to others in writing. And the funny thing about humor is that sometimes it isn't immediately obvious. Sometimes it requires distance and perspective—and a knowledge of the backstory. This is "situational humor," and it's great fun to write about.

The "Hare-y" Part

Every December, John's amateur theatrical group—twenty or so creative, funny actors and stage crew, along with spouses from all walks of life—gathered at the spacious home of one of its members. There, we celebrated that year's successful theatrical productions with a covered dish dinner, sparkling conversation, liberal libation, and a game called Yankee Swap. It was the social highlight of our holiday season—and for some of us, the entire year.

The rules of Yankee Swap were simple: each person or couple brought a ten dollar present; funny or gag gifts were encouraged. Flea market finds, weird attic treasures, and quirky retro discards were popular. Wrapped and without nametags, they were piled at the end of the great room where we gathered. Couples or individuals drew numbers from a basket—from one to twenty or however many people were present. The person or couple who drew number one chose a gift, unwrapped it, and held it up for all to see. Then the person who drew number two could pick a new gift or "steal" a previously opened gift. The person they "stole" it from could choose a new one. And so on in numerical order.

One year we came home with a hideous vase, which we were tempted to drop into the dumpster at the end of the road, but instead we wrapped and regifted it the following year. Another time we were the proud recipients of a scrawny, rubber, stuffed chicken that squawked when it was squeezed. We learned through the years to go "small" when choosing, as they were easier to dispose of.

Sometimes we got lucky and opened our gift to discover food such as cheeses or nuts or a box of candy—and tried to hide it so that someone else wouldn't steal it when it was their turn. The most coveted number was one, since that person went both first and last and had the pick of all previously opened gifts.

One year, thanks to Mike's "Roadkill" episode, it occurred to me that the perfect gift lay in our bottom desk drawer. It was unique, disgusting, and definitely a conversation piece. If ever there was a group with a sense of humor, it was this one. So I wrapped the place mats in red tissue paper and placed them in a festive gift bag, confident they would be a hit.

As usual, it was a rousing party, and when it was game time, John and I were lucky enough to snag the best seats in the house—front row center beside our friends Phyllis and Tom. One by one, the creative actor types chose and revealed their gifts, often with hilarious, award-worthy reactions.

After Harry opened a box to find a very convincing miniature human skull, he held it high and professed, "Alas poor Yorick! I knew him, Horatio ...."

The group was halfway through the pile, and our gift had not yet been claimed when it was Phyllis and Tom's turn. Tom stood and headed straight for our gift bag. I saw John stiffen, then he squeezed my arm—discreetly because, as I said, our seats were in full view of everyone.

Tom handed the prize to his wife, and as she tore away the red paper, it suddenly hit me as the theme from *Jaws* came to mind from nowhere!

This was not going to be pretty.

To say that Phyllis was an animal lover would be like saying, "Kids tolerate ice cream." She had a house full of dogs and was active on the show circuit. She belonged to K9 clubs and was involved in rescues—and was a member of PETA in good standing. In short, Phyllis's life revolved around animals.

She held the pack of place mats at arm's length. Then, with her glasses on, she tilted her head to the side, squinted, and rotated the mats. Gradually her eyes widened, and there was a pained expression on her face—as though someone had shot a staple into her temple. As I've said, there were approximately twenty pairs of eyes on us. We didn't dare look at each other. Just our luck. The one person in the room who should *not* receive a picture of a "sail bunny" was staring at it as though it were a human head on a spike.

Personally, I was torn between a desire to laugh hysterically (as a few others were doing) and a concern that our friend appeared to be somewhere between a cardiac event and a fit of apoplexy. But my primary concern was sitting a mere ten inches away. My husband, who, as you might recall, is a chronic "truth-teller" and would rather be run over by an eighteen-wheeler than tell a lie. So I gave him the "hairy eyeball" warning: *"Do not, under any circumstances, reveal that we brought this tasteless gift!"* And, sure enough, not only did he get it, his acting skills kicked in full force. The next thing I knew, he was shaking his head and adopting a tsk-tsk expression that matched mine.

"Oh, this is terrible! I can't look at it ...," Phyllis said, making no attempt to hide her revulsion. Giving me a sideways glance, she whispered, "What kind of a person ...?" She shoved the offensive place mats toward her husband as people laughed and someone hummed "Here Comes Peter Cottontail." One person even applauded.

So my thoughtful and quick-thinking husband said the only comforting thing he could think of. And really, it saved the day.

"Pass them around, Tom. Maybe somebody else will choose them." So Tom did just that, and sure enough, theatrical types, it seems, do have a high tolerance for gore and carnage. Not only did someone steal them from Phyllis, they were stolen at least once again.

John always chooses a gift for us and got lucky that year—a round can with four flavors of delicious popcorn.

When the game ended, we adjourned for dessert. But Phyllis wasn't up to digesting food. Just as well, as the centerpiece was everyone's favorite: a large, decorated, multilayered carrot cake.

On the way home, John asked, "Did you notice who ended up with the place mats?" To which I responded, "No, but next year be sure to choose something *really small* when it's your turn!"

That was fifteen years ago, and we have never come clean or been outed. To this day, no one knows our little secret—that we were the gifters of tasteless carnage. From time to time when we're in the company of old friends from the play group—more often than not, at a funeral or memorial service—Phyllis will recall the infamous place mats, and it's always with a shudder of revulsion.

I realize we're blowing our cover now and possibly damaging our reputations forever, but really, how likely is Phyllis to read a story titled "Roadkill"?

≪ ● ≫

Family remains an endless source of material for this writer. I was in the fitness center the other day watching an interview with Mike. I nearly fell off the elliptical when he said, "I actually enjoy all the traveling I do for work. Our parents never took us anywhere when we were growing up. No vacations or trips...."

As soon as I left the gym, I called him. "Really," I said. "You make your father and me sound like...like absentee parents...like we deprived our children."

"Sorry, Mom, but honestly that's how I remember it. I mean, where did we ever go?"

He had a point, but I needed to tell him my side of the story. So I sat down and wrote this letter.

"Like Normal Families"

Mike,

I'm sending you this story to remind you why we didn't take vacations like normal families. Our last family trip was exactly fifty years ago. Let me refresh your memory. You were nine.

I'm dedicating this story to Dad because he was the only one who had the good sense to vote against the trip, which was all your fault by the way. It was *your* best friend whose family invited us.

You thought you were so clever, telling your little brothers about the invitation before you told us. And in retrospect, I guess you were. Naturally, they ran into the kitchen squealing, "Can we go? Huh? Can we go? It's going to be so much fun. Three days at the ocean, a swimming pool, a tent. Can we? Puh-*leeease*?!"

"Well...," I said. "Let's go in and see what Dad thinks."

Your father lowered his newspaper and stared at me as though I had suggested spending three days at the Chicago stockyards and slaughterhouse. "Let me get this straight," he said. "You want us to ride 250 miles with the same two kids who threw up on the one-mile drive to church last Sunday?"

"Well, it's not like they didn't have coffee cans," I said.

Your father was emphasizing every syllable, as though I were a lip-reader. *"So that we can sleep in a tent ... on the sand ... in Virginia ... in August ... ! It'll be a blast furnace, Peg."*

Your father worked *one* summer at Bethlehem Steel, so naturally he's an expert on heat.

"A blast furnace with mosquitoes and flies and gnats. Surely you're kidding!"

"Uh ... let Dad and me talk about it," I said. "You guys go outside and play for a while."

Your father dropped the paper and held out his hands like St. Peter welcoming me through the pearly gates. "We have paradise right here, Peg—a flowing stream with sand, a small forest, a field, pets, and they're building a new YMCA family center right around the corner. What more could a kid ask for?"

Quite a lot, apparently, if the shouts coming through the open windows were any indication. "Yippee! We're going to the ocean! To sleep in a tent! On the sand! And cook hamburgers over an open fire! Like normal kids! It's what I always dreamed of doing—before I die."

"Oh, John," I said, "every child should dig a hole in the sand and see the ocean come up, catch a fish from a pier, and experience grit in his bathing suit. Pulling to the shoulder to dump puke from sloshing coffee cans is a small price to pay. We'll only be there for two full days. Let's do it, hon. Let's have some fun!"

St. Peter knew when he was beat.

I could have gotten medication for your brothers' motion sickness—something to put them to sleep for the four-hour trip, but as tempting as that was, it sounded extreme. Yet when we were a good twenty miles from home and keeping an eye on the Johnson's car pulling the pop-up camper ahead, it happened. You wouldn't remember that, Mike, because you weren't in the barf mobile. You were riding with Jack—having fun. Well, I'm here to tell you, nothing sucks the joy from a road trip like the sound of vomit splashing into coffee cans in the back seat.

For three hours, we played games and sang every song I could think of. Had I known that this would be the highlight of our trip, I'd have put more into it. It was evening by the time we arrived at the campsite to the sound of ocean waves and mosquitos the size of dune buggies.

Memories of that three-day vacation fifty years ago still resurface from time to time—kind of like the recurrence of malaria symptoms. *"It's like a sauna out here.... There's sand in my mouth .... There's sand in my sleeping bag .... There's sand in my underpants...."*

The following morning as we were having breakfast in the blast furnace, four-year-old Phil brought his egg and bacon sandwich to me.

"It's all gritty, Mommy," he whined, spitting a mouthful onto his plate.

Six-year-old Scott, whose quick wit had blossomed at a young age, reminded him, "Well, it *is* a *sand*wich."

Minutes later, we left the mosquitos and flies and gnats and oppressive humidity behind and headed across the burning sand to the cool, frothy ocean waves. A half hour or so later, as I was calling your fair-skinned four-year-old brother in from the sun, a monstrous wave from behind flattened and dragged him along the bottom. He surfaced holding his ears.

After that, it was the screaming I remember. It continued throughout the ten-mile ambulance trip to the hospital. Well, except for the two minutes Phil was busy throwing up in my lap. We were the only vehicle on the road, except for Dad who was following in our car. Still, the driver turned on the deafening siren. Who could blame him? Again, you wouldn't remember any of this, Mike, as you and Scott had stayed behind with the Johnsons to enjoy the ocean, pool, and arcade. What followed still gives me nightmares.

Walking into the ER was like stepping onto the set of a futuristic movie: spotless, sterile surfaces, nurses and doctors in crisp white uniforms, and everywhere refreshing cool air with the faint odor of disinfectant. Not a mosquito, fly, or gnat in sight—just a four-year-old sitting on the edge of the examining table rubbing the mosquito bites that peppered his arms and legs. The only sand there was fell from his matted, curly hair onto a face and shoulders pink from the sun and sticky with lotion.

His crying turned to sobs as he was distracted by the hustle and bustle around him.

Standing there in our wet bathing suits, old T-shirts, and flip-flops, your father and I looked like a couple of refugees who just swam to freedom. The sour stench of vomit wafted from my shirt as your father gave me a half smile. He wasn't fooling me. I knew what he was thinking: *are we having fun yet?*

Anyway, Mike, as soon as the black grit was flushed from your brother's ears, his sobbing stopped. Minutes later, he was licking an orange popsicle and swinging his legs while a pretty young nurse applied cool compresses and soothing lotion to his shoulders and back.

Your father nudged me and said under his breath, "He looks like a prospector who's hit the mother lode."

And then your little brother—the same one who's normally terrified of doctors and hospitals—said to your father and me, "I should probably stay here. I don't mind. You can pick me up tomorrow."

Before I could offer to stay with him, your father spoke up. "Oh no, you don't. If I have to go back there, *we're all going.*"

"We'll get in the pool this afternoon," I promised, as we headed back to our one-star waterfront resort.

Surely you remember the next part, Mike. We arrived at poolside in time to hear screams of horror. *"Oooh, look! Somebody's pooped in the swimming pool, and it's floating around like a little brown buoy!"*

"It's a *poo-y!*" Scott declared.

Whatever the technical term, it cleared the pool quicker than a jagged bolt of lightning—for the rest of the day. Which was unfortunate as a rip tide had closed the beach.

The following morning, before the rains began in earnest, your father joined Mr. Johnson in the shallow creek nearby. Side by side, barefoot, and holding a dip net and fishing lines with chicken necks at the end, they set about catching crabs for our dinner. I'd never noticed before, but apparently Dad's big toe bears a strong resemblance to a chicken neck, and ... well, let's just say his scream wasn't quite as loud as your brother's.

And you wonder why we didn't travel with you kids? Call us a couple of cowards, Mike, but your father and I adopted Dorothy Gale's philosophy after that trip: there really is *no place like home.*

Later that year we joined the new YMCA Family Center down the street—with two swimming pools. Maybe you could mention that on one of your interviews.

Chapter 12

FAMILY TIES

JOHN AND I ARE NORMAL PARENTS. WE'RE PROUD OF our children and treasure our time with them. We try not to take it personally that they've moved thousands of miles away. The good news is, we've tracked them down. In fact, we've gone to work with our engineer son and watched him drill for core samples and water. We've sat behind his office desk, seen a reservoir and tunnel under construction, and enjoyed a hands-on tour of his lab. We've visited another son's secondhand bookstore and left with armloads of delightful, out-of-print reading material as well as applauded his performances at theatrical productions. That said, I respect their privacy and try not to intrude into their adult personal lives with my writing.

Son Mike is a different story altogether. He's already out there in public view, so to speak. I figure that anyone who has inseminated a pig, combed hippopotamus poop from his hair, and bitten the testicles off a baby lamb in front of millions of people is fair game for his mother's stories. His career has given us a glimpse into a world most people never see. We've joined him on episodes of *Dirty Jobs* and *Somebody's Gotta Do It* as well as a half dozen or so television commercials for Viva Paper Towels, Lee Jeans, Fel-Pro Gaskets, and various cleaning products.

When CNN invited my husband and me to New York City for a live interview to promote Mike's new show, we were tempted. It was 2015, and *Somebody's Gotta Do It* was in full production. John and I were familiar with the show; we had even made guest appearances on a couple of fun episodes.

Our only reservation was the actual travel. We are not fans of trains and planes, so when CNN offered to send a car to Baltimore *and* put us up in a suite at a nearby five-star hotel, we took our suitcases from the closet.

"Strangers in a Strange Land"

This wasn't our first trip to the Big Apple. Back in the mid-nineties, when Mike's TV career was still in the early stages and before he was a celebrity, he worked in New

York City where he shared an apartment with a married friend whose wife was working on the West Coast. For Christmas one year, while his friend was traveling, he invited us for our first-ever visit to New York City—with all the bells and whistles.

After a four-hour bus trip, we headed for Mike's apartment. Less than a minute after we stepped from our taxi in front of the Beaumont, the doorman ran out to greet us. "Mr. and Mrs. Rowe! Welcome!" he said, grabbing our bags.

We stared at the uniformed man. The Beaumont was an enormous establishment—31 stories and over 150 apartments. With so many residents, how in the world did he know who we were? He read our minds.

"Your son gave me a description and asked me to be on the lookout. 'Their mouths will be gaping, and they'll be staring up at the tall buildings,' Mike said. I recognized you right away."

For two country folks who avoided crowds of people with the same fervor they avoided swarms of hornets, New York City was an eye-opener indeed. Our son graciously gave up his comfortable waterbed and slept in his friend's bed. The ironing board that was a permanent fixture in his bedroom made a convenient valet for our clothes—and I soon recovered from the shock of a refrigerator that was as empty as it was on the day it was delivered, except for some bottled water.

A view of Central Park—and a skyline the likes of which we had seen only in pictures—had us glued to the apartment windows in wonder.

Mike was our tour guide, planning each activity and shepherding us about the city like a dedicated border collie. One minute he was prodding us along so as not to be late for a Broadway show or the Radio City Music Hall, the next, he was feeding us at such landmarks as Cafe Mozart for breakfast, Fraunces Tavern for lunch, and Tavern On the Green for dinner. John was in awe at the American Museum of Natural History (AMNH) and amazed by the *Pile of Dirt with Shovel* exhibit in the Museum of Modern Art.

"Geez, Mike," he said, "they call that art? Maybe I could interest them in a pile of horse manure and a pitchfork." We laughed as the art connoisseurs nearby looked down their noses at us. Not everyone has an appreciation for art—or a sense of humor.

The floor of the New York Stock Exchange on Wall Street was hallowed ground to my husband. He'd had a longtime crush on a host at The Business Channel. He denied it, of course, but a wife can tell. He watched the show as religiously as he attended church and was far more attentive to her than he was to our minister. Now he was looking around hopefully.

"Come on, John," I said. "She's not here."

"I don't know what you're talking about," he replied, with an innocent look.

By the time we visited the World Trade Center and St. Patrick's Cathedral, he had forgotten all about her. I think.

To his credit, not once did our son show the stress he must have felt showing two unpredictable, wide-eyed tourists a good time while keeping them safe in the big city. Of course, we wouldn't tell Mike about our "real adventure" until much later.

It happened the evening he surprised us with a Broadway show, sharing with us beforehand only that it was a musical. I knew little about the Broadway scene but had heard about the popular revivals and was imagining *Oklahoma!* or *South Pacific* or *Carousel*. What fun!

John and I had spent the afternoon at the AMNH and arrived back at the Beaumont barely in time to be hurried into a cab and whisked off to the Ambassador Theatre in Midtown Manhattan.

Had I not been preoccupied in prayer and holding on for dear life during the cab ride, I would have been obsessing about the fact that there hadn't been time to change from our jeans, tennis shoes, and casual jackets.

The driver, totally immersed in an animated personal telephone conversation, drove erratically, bouncing the cab off a curb—twice. Finally, our son yelled, "Stop!" several blocks short of our destination, and we got out—whereupon Mike (famous for his generosity) remarked that it was the first time ever he had not tipped a driver.

The musical was called *Bring in 'da Noise, Bring in 'da Funk,* and for the first few minutes, our mouths gaped. Now and then my husband and I exchanged quick glances and chuckled. Of course, in no time, we were thoroughly immersed and tapping our feet. Turns out we were over-dressed. Except, of course, for the woman across the aisle wearing a long, black sequined gown.

After the show, Mike announced that the three of us were invited to a party down the street. As it was after 11 p.m. and we'd had a full day, we opted to get a cab and head back to the apartment.

"Go to your party," we told Mike. "Have a good time. We'll be fine."

It was a brisk, cheerful evening, as bright as midday and sidewalks teemed with people in a festive mood. Best of all, Christmas was in the air, so instead of hailing a cab, we began walking the thirteen blocks. Feeling like a couple of kids away from parental scrutiny for the first time in days, we stopped at a small café. What fun! When we finished eating, we put on our coats and started back to Mike's apartment—heading *in the wrong direction.*

After ten blocks or so, we realized our mistake, turned around, and walked the twenty-some blocks back to the Beaumont. Not once did we feel uneasy or threatened, just exhausted. The following morning when we had a hard time getting out of bed, Mike apologized for the demanding schedule and promised to give us a break.

Our current 2015 visit to New York City was quite different. CNN put us up in the fancy Trump Tower where we spent the first hour counting all the objects in our room that bore the Trump name or logo—candy bars, water bottles, soaps, lotions, shampoos, slippers, robes, towels ... The smaller items became souvenirs for friends on both sides of the political spectrum. Then we headed across the street for a walk in the famous Central Park, amazed at the number of children playing there. One doesn't think of children living in New York City. And so many dogs with dog walkers. A decade after our first visit, we still stood out as gawking tourists.

On the morning of our interview with Brooke Baldwin, we rose early, dressed, and headed for a leisurely breakfast. No hurry since Mike was already at the studio shooting promo ads.

We were coming down to the lobby when John walked to the back of the elevator, which was empty except for us—or so I thought.

As you've probably heard, my husband chats with strangers on elevators, and I feared he had gone round the bend when he turned and said to no one, "So where's a good place to eat breakfast in this town?"

"John," I said, as we reached the first floor and the doors opened. "Who are you ... ?" And that's when a slender middle-aged man in jeans, T-shirt, and a baseball cap emerged from the dark corner of the elevator and walked past me, saying, "Right through those doors, sir."

John thanked him, and we headed toward the street.

"No!" the man called, coming after us. He pointed to the hotel restaurant across the room. "Those doors."

"Oh, it's too late. They're closing soon," John said.

"Wait right here," the man told us before hurrying into the restaurant. Seconds later, he reappeared and motioned us through the doors, saying, "It's OK, they're still serving."

We thanked him and were seated at a table for two while the man in the ball cap headed to the back of the restaurant. We were reading the menu when a wide-eyed woman at the table beside us leaned over and said, "Do you know who that man is?"

"What man?" I asked.

"The man you came in with."

We shook our heads no, and her eyes sparkled. "That was Bruce Willis!" she said, clearly anxious to see our reactions. "He owns a penthouse apartment in this hotel!"

"Really?" I said. "He didn't look like Bruce Willis."

Her husband looked at us and smiled. "Oh, you can take her word for it. Believe me, my wife is an expert when it comes to celebrities."

"That's because he has lost weight and has a cap on," the woman added. "Demi Moore is here too. His ex. Their daughter is opening in a play tonight." She sounded like one of those *TMZ Hollywood* gossip reporters, and I didn't doubt her for a moment.

She leaned in again pointing to two men having breakfast at a nearby table. "Do you know who he is?" She nodded toward a bushy-browed man who looked vaguely familiar.

I shook my head. "No clue."

She straightened and smiled broadly. "That's Martin Scorsese, the famous Hollywood filmmaker!"

"Really? Impressive!" I said. Then I looked up and saw the man who had shown us into the restaurant— possibly Bruce Willis. He was walking toward our table. I could hear the celebrity-watcher gasp as Mr. Willis placed a book on the table in front of John. It was a Zagat Restaurant Guide for New York City.

"Here you go, sir. This book might come in handy while you're in New York. It's a big town."

My husband jumped up and shook the man's hand. "I'm sorry I didn't recognize you, Bruce. My wife and I don't go to the movies very often."

"Oh, that's OK," he said while smiling. I'm thinking we probably reminded him of his parents.

Next thing I knew I was on my feet saying something stupid like, "But we enjoyed *Moonlighting* back in the '80s. Oh yeah, and we loved *The Sixth Sense*!"

Then Bruce Willis saw Martin Scorsese and politely excused himself. They chatted briefly before he left.

"Gee, hon, that was really something," John said. "This is a nice book. Too bad we're not going to be here longer."

"You should have had Bruce sign it!" the woman beside us chided, but it was too late.

"Hey," John said, when we had finished our breakfast. "Let's go over and ask Martin Sa-sacor'ski if we can take his picture."

"Absolutely not! And it's *Scorsese*," I said. "I am not going to bother that man! John, don't you dare!" But it was too late, of course.

He was very friendly and seemed flattered when John asked if his wife could have her picture taken with him. I was sorry I didn't know more about his career; I would like to have mentioned some movies—or something.

"I'll tell you what!" the man with the eyebrows said. "Don here will take a picture of all three of us. How's that?"

He was delightful, and afterward when I called Mike at CNN to tell him about our brush with two celebrities, he said, "That's great. Send me the picture of you and Marty, and I'll show it to Brooke Baldwin. See you soon."

An hour or so later at CNN we had more brushes with celebrity, including meeting the head honcho, whose name escapes me now, but I'm sure he's very important. The lady in the restaurant would probably know his name.

Brooke Baldwin was gorgeous and charming, and during our interview, said, "I hear you two had a brush with celebrity this morning."

So we told her about Bruce and the next thing we knew, our picture was on the big monitor with Martin

Scorsese—going out to 150 million households, in over 200 countries. Imagine! We felt like genuine celebrities.

It was fun, and everybody loved it. Mike even posted the picture and wrote a story about our celebrity sightings for his millions of FB followers.

He called us later that afternoon with a disturbing question. "What made you think that man was Martin Scorsese?"

"Well, the lady at the next table told us it was. She knew Bruce Willis."

It seems the friendly, bushy-browed gentleman in the restaurant was not Martin Scorsese after all.

CNN had been notified. Possibly by Mr. Scorsese himself, who had called in to set the record straight. About the same time, a woman made an interesting comment beneath the picture on Mike's FB post. "Hey, that's my Uncle George!" Turns out the mystery man was named George Whipple, a bushy-browed NY society reporter.

Anyway, Mike said we managed to set CNN's credibility for fact-checking back light-years.

Chapter 13

MADAM SECRETARY

My friends have known that since college I dabbled in writing. Kind of like they dabbled in crafts, gardening, and tennis. They knew that I wrote poetry for birthdays and anniversaries and eulogies for funerals. But they were not aware of the two children's novels I had written, or the heartache I had experienced while trying to get them published. Or that I had lived with the shame of rejection for much of my adult life—because some things are just too personal, too painful to share, even with good friends. Through the years their passion for tennis and gardening and crafts waned, and they pursued other interests. But I never stopped writing— not really. I had no choice. Through a half century of life— with kids, rejection, cancer, hope, passion, and dreams—I kept writing. Because that's what writers do. They write— whether on paper, a word processor, or in their head.

From time to time in later years, my friends would reach into their purses as we sat at lunch in a restaurant or in our homes and pull out a clipping of my latest news-paper or magazine article—in case I needed an extra copy for an out-of-town relative. They'd chuckle or ask me more about the story. "Is it true? Did you change the names?" I could tell they were proud of my work.

Little did my old teaching buddies know that they had been a source of entertaining material for decades. I'd been taking mental notes at our gatherings and jour-naling the effects of aging on our lives and our friend-ship through the years. And believe me, the stories have never been better. Octogenarian friends are "pure comedy gold!"

From Trish, a widow who's carrying on a steamy romance with her boyfriend from church, to Annie, whose fine dining goes awry when her steamy appetizer dissolves her denture adhesive, to Mary, whose restless husband moves them from home to home, using up an entire page in my address book.

If I have learned anything from our long relationship, it is that the travails of aging are more bearable when shared with friends. And what fun they are to write about. Even if the pieces haven't been published . . . until now.

"Old People"

It's official! According to the *New York Times* Health and Wellness page, my husband reached "old age" some time ago. John strongly resents the sentiment.

"I don't want anybody telling me I'm old," he says. "They don't know me." I don't have to remind him that he's past his sexual peak; I take a gentler approach and retrieve our calendar.

"Here you go, hon. This month's social highlights: senior expo, blood work, a hearing aid evaluation, a dementia seminar at the Department of Aging, a podiatry appointment to get your toenails clipped, a bimonthly lunch date with my old teacher friends, and a dermatology appointment."

Dermatology appointments are the worst. They used to be little more than a drive-through, with a doctor as old as my father peering at me over his glasses and asking, "Anything new I should take a look at . . . ?" Minutes later I'd be on my way with my dignity intact and a complimentary magazine.

Skin checks during COVID-19 had all the elements of a costume party. Me, adorned in socks and a blue tissue paper dress—while my lovely young doctor, armed with a canister of liquid nitrogen, wears a spotlight on her forehead, a magnifying lens in one eye, and a full face mask. At least, I think she was my lovely young dermatologist.

Either way, she was fully prepared to appraise a precious stone, weld a boat propeller, or enter a mine shaft. To her credit, she managed not to gag while examining my skin and bemoaning the tragedy of sun damage. A pretty, masked young blonde assistant documented the proceedings on a tablet, recording measurements and taking pictures—at close range.

Occasionally, I'd pose a silly question such as, "What is this brown spot on my shoulder?" I should know better than to ask. My old doctor used words such as freckles and age spots. This one is full-on medical, spouting terms such as lentigo sinilis or seborrheic keratosis. My husband is convinced that her fee is based on the number of syllables of whatever it is she's removing.

After the ordeal, I'd stagger to the car with extra Band-Aids, gauze, wound care instructions, and an appointment card—another social event for our calendar.

On the Friday evening of a big social event, I was still sporting a burn on my neck and a bandage on my nose from one such appointment. It was our turn to entertain old college friends—six retired schoolteachers still alive and able to hobble to our condominium.

Fifty years ago our little get-togethers began at 8 p.m. with drinks, followed by dinner, a game of charades, laughter, and lively discussions into the wee hours. Everything from current events and politics to our kids' Little League performances, sprinkled with jokes—often risqué. We'd return home in the wee hours, awaken Mom, and walk her across the lawn to her house.

On this Friday, I served dinner at 4:30 p.m., then we sat around sipping non-diuretic drinks and complaining about everything from pacemakers and prostates to colonoscopies and cholesterol. We had a good laugh when Joanne told us about her call to the urology office to make an appointment.

"The secretary asked me to hold, so I told her, 'Hon, if I could hold, I wouldn't be making this call.'"

By 7:00 p.m., our living room looked like the lounge in a nursing home, with guests sprawled across the furniture and nodding off.

We put them on the elevator at 7:30, agreeing that our next get-together—Jack's eighty-eighth birthday celebration—would be over lunch. Our friends tottered to their cars while we waved goodbye from our balcony, grateful that we weren't the ones making the late night trek in the dark.

By 8 p.m., John was in his slippers and ensconced in his domain—a blue leather recliner six feet from the television. To his left were his tablet, a crossword puzzle, and the *TV Guide*. On the right were his flip phone, evening pills, and a bottle of water.

With the drone of the dishwasher in the background, we put our feet up and agreed that there's something to be said for old age.

"Fifty Shades of Gray Matter"

I always look forward to my old teacher luncheons. Never underestimate the value of girlfriends, especially *old* girlfriends. As much as I love the energy and enthusiasm of youth, there's nothing more comforting than a couple of hours with people who remind me of . . . well, me. It's not just about bodies that mirror my own—sagging, wrinkled skin, nonexistent waistlines, and gray hair (except for Dora's; she colors hers, but you didn't hear it from me). Old friends give me permission to be myself—to act my age, as it were. Put simply, I feel normal when I'm with them. And when their wrinkles are deeper than mine or their skin flabbier, I love them all the more.

It was that time of the month again—for six decrepit old classmates and teaching colleagues to meet for lunch. With all of us still married to our college sweethearts, we had well over a half century of history and memories. I've come to think of these gatherings as group therapy.

We'd come a long way since being on extended maternity leave together. That was back when we met in our homes with as many as fifteen kids in tow. Kids who were devoted to wrecking our playrooms while we moms spread peanut butter and jelly and slapped bologna and cheese sandwiches together at the kitchen counter.

Our luncheons are way more civilized now. Like our recent gathering at a lovely old country tavern.

It was a Wednesday morning when I backed my car into a parking spot at the shopping center where I was to meet Annie. I'd driven the previous time, as Annie had been suffering from a bout of what she called traffic anxiety.

It was a big day for my friend—her geriatric trifecta. She was sporting new dentures, new hearing aids, and new bifocals. But when she told me it was her first time behind the wheel of their new car, I opened the door and told her I was driving.

"No, no, I've got this," she said. "Close that door! Besides, I have to learn some time, right? Ben won't let me drive when we're together; apparently, I make him…anxious. Men!"

If this was aimed at reassuring me, it missed the mark. Too nervous to talk, Annie was hunched low, her knuckles white against the steering wheel, her eyes laser-focused on the road ahead. For the next twenty minutes, I plied my navigator skills, concentrating on the speed limit and traffic, looking for the defroster and windshield wipers, and giving directions.

From time to time, I made reassuring comments such as, "You're doing great, Annie. Really! I'm so proud of you! You haven't hit one pedestrian or been pulled over for speeding." We were going 15 in a 45-mph zone.

Annie and I had arrived at the restaurant and joined the others when Dora came rushing in, looking frazzled.

"I was vacuuming this morning and lost track of time," she told us. "When I saw the clock, I panicked and jumped right in the shower." She picked up her menu and gave a little giggle. "Fortunately, I vacuum in the nude."

"What?" I asked. "You mean, *nothing* on?"

"I do it all the time—well, since the kids left home."

"You were home alone, right?" one of the girls asked.

"No, Dan was in the next room. Sometimes he joins me in the shower afterward."

When we laughed, Dora, who had put on some weight through the years, added, "Hey, my body might not be perfect these days, but it is what it is." Nobody laughed harder than Dora, who clearly enjoyed her story as much as the rest of us. Our therapy session had begun.

Every successful support group has a facilitator. Lucille keeps things rolling for us, making sure everyone has a turn to share as we make our way through a delicious lunch that we didn't have to prepare. She went first, and when she struggled to remember the name of her cousin, then couldn't remember the name of the grocery store where she's been shopping twice a week for the past thirty years, I wanted to shout a triumphant "Yes!" It was all so wickedly comforting. We sympathized over her husband's lymphedema and shook our heads over her sciatica.

When Dora paused in the story about her granddaughter's graduation and said, "What was I just talking about?" we all laughed. And when she shared her distress over her struggling, divorced son who had lost his job, our sympathy and concern were genuine—as well as our relief that it wasn't our own son experiencing such hardship.

We were slurping soup as Mary told us about her upcoming vacation with twelve in-laws and speculated as to whether or not they'd still be on speaking terms at the end of the week. Then she talked about her female issues and impending surgery.

"I don't know why our body parts can't just stay put!" she said. We're all waiting to see how successful her surgery is before we ask for her doctor's number.

For some reason, Annie lost her appetite after her crab soup and put the rest of her lunch in a doggie bag for later.

"Are you nervous about making that left-hand turn out of the parking lot, Annie?" I whispered. "Because we can always turn right and go down to the traffic light."

"No, no, I just had a big breakfast," she said.

Annie had brought me a newspaper clipping of my latest essay in the *Baltimore Sun*, prompting questions about my writing routine. So I answered them all—but good. "I write through the morning until early afternoon. From time to time I stop writing, get up from my computer, and bounce a big ball against the wall a couple of hundred times. You know, overhand, underarm, sidearm . . . while I march in place. It's great exercise! Sometimes I do it three times a day."

"But . . . you live in a condominium," somebody said. "Aren't you afraid your neighbors will hear you?"

"I hope they do," I said. "I want them to think we're having rough sex."

We were all laughing as I explained that rough sex means you're awake for it.

When we finished, figuring our bills and tips took a good fifteen minutes and Trish finding her car keys, another five. She looked everywhere and finally dumped the contents of her purse onto the table so that we could all help. No car keys. At that point, Lucille remembered that Trish had ridden with her.

After we looked at our calendars and chose a date for the next get-together, we rose to leave, standing in place a minute or so until our joints creaked into motion.

On our way home, after successfully negotiating the left hand turn out of the parking lot, Annie confided in me.

"Peggy! That hot crab soup dissolved my denture adhesive, and I can't chew!"

"I thought you were quiet," I said. "Take them out so we can talk."

She did. "I'm starved! We're stopping at the dairy for a milkshake on the way home."

Honestly! Who needs therapy when we have old friends?

"Update—Fifty Shades of Even Grayer Matter"
Sadly, our group of six has diminished to five decrepit old teachers limping to our bimonthly luncheon/therapy session—two of us on canes and three of us widowed.

Nevertheless, here we were again—in a dark corner booth this time—bonding over pizza, salad, crab soup, and hamburgers. On today's agenda: hip, kneecap, and cataract surgeries; the ineffectiveness of hearing aids, bathing suits, and varicose veins; and the annoying phenomenon of prolapse.

And here is the best part: Trish, a widow in our group, is dating a widower friend from her church and has livened our conversations. Actually, she provides us with all the excitement we can handle. The octogenarian version of *Fifty Shades of Grey,* we heard about church dinner dates, hand-holding during the Sunday sermon, hugging and kissing while watching sporting events on TV, and—hold on to your hat—a timeshare in the Bahamas *and* an upcoming European cruise! Yikes! My glasses fogged up just listening.

Well, you know how writers are. It was the elephant in the room, so why not?

"Trish," I said to my old friend, "are you and Mac living in sin?"

She laughed. "Oh, Peggy, believe me, very little sinning goes on when you're in your eighties."

I can't wait until our next luncheon. A geriatric support group with PG-13 entertainment. It really doesn't get any better. I only wish I could talk Trish into taking notes.

I must admit, the visual of vacuuming in the nude has stayed with me. Maybe it's not such a bad idea. Maybe I should put it all out there like Dora and share my writing journey—the potholes and detours, the tears and shame of rejection, and the amazing scenery along the way. Hey, it is what it is.

Chapter 14

THE BOOK IN THE DRAWER

IT WAS 2016, AND MY TWO MIDDLE GRADE/YOUNG adult novels were still safely sequestered in my bottom desk drawer like treasured family heirlooms. And where they would probably remain until the children disposed of our belongings someday—along with our ashes. I thought about the estate auctions my husband and I had enjoyed early in our marriage, where I had opened old furniture drawers to discover personal letters and children's photographs once treasured by a loved one. I wondered if my books would meet the same fate. I had long since given up on seeing them in print.

I was somewhat comforted by a favorite trope trotted out by presenters at conferences: "Oh yes," they'd say, smiling, "*The book in the drawer*. Every successful writer has a *book in the drawer*. Think of it as your 'learning tool.' You tried, you made mistakes, and you've learned more than you realize from writing that book." Maybe my books in the drawer were like the blouse I made in home ec with the uneven sleeves that fell off when it was washed, or the lopsided sconce our son made in shop and proudly presented to me. Not perfect perhaps, but learning tools—and the result of great effort.

Perhaps I was ahead of the game with *two* learning tools in my drawer. One of my manuscripts had seen the light of day, ever so briefly, several years earlier when Mike lugged it all the way to New York City with him and handed it to a publisher he was meeting—in person. An editor read parts of it and had some nice things to say about my writing, but in the end, deemed my protagonist not as sympathetic as I had hoped.

Still, writing filled my life, and though I still dreamed of publishing a book, there was satisfaction in seeing my essays and stories in newspapers and magazines. Mike routinely told me, "Just keep writing, Mom. Who knows, maybe you're writing a book right now. Your stories are great."

To this day, people—writers especially—are curious to know how I finally managed to break through the "iron dome" of the book publishing world in my dotage. "It's a long story," I tell them. "Pull up a chair …."

"Just a Growing-Up Story"

Do not underestimate the power of guilt. When your three sons have moved as far away from home as they can get and still live in the United States of America, there's nothing wrong with a well-placed email reminding them that many years ago you endured the agony of childbirth to give them life—and that you're still alive and kicking should they feel the urge to call you. (It doesn't hurt to insert your phone number, just in case.)

Thanks to technology, it's easy to keep our three kids up to date on all things Dad and Mom. There have been regular phone calls, texts, and emails to my offspring. They so look forward to each and every one—Lord knows, I would hate to disappoint them!

One day, out of pure frustration with my stubborn husband, I vented by shooting off a text to our firstborn. I was in no mood to check for typos—which was unusual for me. That very evening, John and I were sitting in a theater during intermission when Mike texted me a link to his Facebook page. "Check this out," he said. I did, and lo and behold, he had shared my personal, typo-ridden venting text with his millions of fans. I quickly got over my initial embarrassment after reading some of the thousands of comments. Readers found my post hilarious—many of them expressing concern that my husband's prostate was lying on a scorching sidewalk somewhere in Baltimore.

Here is the embarrassing text.

> *Mike,*
> *You fathers out walking,*
> *And it's 93 degrees. I couldn't*

> *talk him out of it. So I told him*
> *to make sure he has his ID on*
> *him so that they can call me from*
> *the hospital. He's wearing his*
> *sunglasses because they make*
> *him look sexy. I reminded him*
> *that lying prostate on the sidewalk*
> *is never sexy no matter what your*
> *wearing. If he is still alive, we're*
> *going to the theater tonight to*
> *see Sister Act.*

A couple of days later, Mike called. "Hey, Mom, I think we might be onto something here. Send me another text next week, and we'll see what happens." A week later, after Mike returned from the road, I sent him another.

> *Home from NY yet, Mike? Get this.*
> *Your father wants to go to Northern Scotland—*
> *on our own—rent a car... We are people who*
> *get lost in Baltimore! And they drive on*
> *the left! I told Dad we're not going*
> *anywhere until he has that hernia repaired.*
> *It's making eerie groaning sounds.*
> *Along with his squeaky foot brace and*
> *squealing hearing aids, he's like a*
> *one-man band. Stay tuned. Call soon.*

This text was even more popular than the first, so, per Mike's request, I wrote him a humorous story in the form of a letter, then another. Read by Mike with pure joy, they received the same enthusiastic responses. The comments written to Mike by his fans were full of advice and every bit as entertaining as my letters. Especially the cautionary ones warning Mike of our impending demise.

I've included a few of my favorites.

Donna O: "Mike, cherish your parents while they are here. One day you'll turn around, and they'll be gone."

Dan: "Mike, you have such a nice bond with your parents. You will crave them when they have passed."

Alexander P: "Their stories are so funny, Mike. Enjoy them while they are still alive—before their minds go."

Connie: "Love your parents, Mike. You never know when the Lord will be taking them home."

And then one day, a dreadful occurrence! I left my blue purse—containing my wallet and cell phone (in short, my life)—dangling from the handle of a shopping cart in the Walmart parking lot. After somewhat recovering from a brief nervous breakdown, I called and shared my angst with the children; I needed sympathy. Two of them provided it.

But not Mike. "Don't *tell* me about it, Mom," he said. "Sit down and write about it—in a letter to me. Email it soon; I'm on the road tomorrow evening for a few days."

So while the details were painfully fresh, I did just that, then hit the "Send" button. I called my story "Old Blue." Mike read it aloud, recorded it, and shared the video on his Facebook page before leaving town. It went viral, ended up on YouTube, and by the time Mike returned, it had been viewed seventy million times. But the truly exciting part was yet to come. Days later, *real* publishers from *big* publishing houses reached out to Mike, suggesting that if his mother were to write a couple of dozen humorous stories about *him* in the same vein, they would publish them in a book—in a heartbeat. Because, as we all know— celebrity sells!

So of course, I sat right down and wrote a humorous book. But not about my son. I wrote instead about growing up with the most interesting character I have ever known: my mother, Thelma Knobel. Many of the stories I had already written because, as I've said, my mother was such a compelling character, and writers simply can't *not* write. I had attended a writing seminar at my alma mater (now Towson University) years earlier where I submitted a humorous story about my mother.

A creative writing professor read it and gave me a one-on-one critique—one that has lived in my mind to this day. "Peggy, I have to tell you right up front—*I am in love with your mother!* Seriously," he said, "what a delightful character! And you have portrayed her beautifully." I especially loved his final comment: "Peggy, you should consider writing a book about growing up with her—a mother/daughter story."

And now, I was doing just that. I finished my book in February 2017 while visiting our son's family in Florida. I chose a prominent editor, one I had met and observed at writers' conferences. An editor who insisted on a hard copy, the old-fashioned way—so I followed the rules as I had all those years ago, and my daughter-in-law, Marjie, printed it out for me. The editor responded weeks later. His first paragraph brought goose bumps.

"First of all, let me say how much I enjoy your writing, and your sense of humor. At its best this material skirts between the darkness of sarcasm and the lightness of a big heart and a wonderful story about a mother and a daughter. You are clearly a writer of much skill and talent."

His second paragraph gave me chest pains.

"Now, let me tell you what's wrong with your book." And boy, did he tell me. As it stood, my book was neither a collection of stories nor was it a memoir. There was no through line that builds to a fiery climax, no extreme situation, no chapters that stood alone—with a beginning, a middle, and an end. There was very little at stake, and no villain.

What followed brought bile to my throat and reprised the hopelessness I'd experienced all those years ago when submitting my children's novels. The editor had seen the video of Mike reading "Old Blue" on social media and loved it. So much so that he gave me the following advice: "That story about losing your purse made me think that perhaps you should really just do a collection of short stories that Mike reads first and then gets collected into a book. Maybe you do ten of them to begin with. That way you'll have his social media platform to fall back on."

I saw his critique as a prediction of failure from the get-go. And yet, I refrained from jumping from our balcony (like I could even make it over the railing) or overdosing on my cholesterol medication. I forwarded the critique to Mike in an email. My note said it all.

*On Mon, Mar 6, 2017, at 11:48 AM, Peggy
Rowe < > wrote: Hi Mike. Well, it's official. Your
mother is a skilled writer with a great talent
for writing garbage. But that's okay because I'll
always have your social media platform to fall
back on. I'm not sure how to proceed—maybe
just forget writing and grow old-er gracefully,
playing mah-jongg and singing in the church
choir. Just kidding, of course. I'm fine. I just need
some time to think and stop feeling sorry for
myself. Mom*

Of course, I hadn't even gotten to the editor's actual
chapter-by-chapter critique with suggestions on how to
make my book work as a memoir.

In the meantime, my friend Michele asked me several
times if she could read my book. She offered to give
me her opinion as an editor and writer. But instead of
sending her my book, I revisited the first editor's chapter
suggestions—agreeing with many of them. Especially
the one I saw over and over: "Make a scene, for Pete's
sake! Stop *telling* me! *Show* me!" I worked until I felt
hopeful again, and then I reread the editor's paragraph
about falling back on my son's social media platform and
lost my confidence. The book was worthless.

Later, I was having lunch with Michele one day
when she finally convinced me to let her read the book
that was causing me such angst. Two weeks later we met
again. She looked me in the eye and said, "Peggy, this
book is fucking hilarious!" Or something like that. "I'm
your friend; I will always tell you the truth!" So we did
some light revision and line edits, and when we finished,

I sent it off to Mike, who then forwarded it to publishers, while I prayed.

They responded quickly. There was *no* interest! The general feeling was: "Nobody knows your mother, Mike, and nobody has ever heard of your grandmother. It would be a *tough sell.*"

It was far from my first rejection, but this one felt especially cruel, as I had foolishly allowed myself to dream—once again. Oh yeah, despite the popular song of the 1930s, we *never* grow too old to dream. Those feelings of not measuring up and of being an outsider resurfaced. *There would be no book!* Not back then, not today, and not in the future. Of that, I was certain.

I was wrong.

<< ◆ >>

At this point, Mike took time from his hectic production schedule to read my manuscript . . . from cover to cover . . . for the first time. His heartwarming comment to me was as good as having it published—almost. I so respect him as a writer.

"Mom, this book is *terrific*! It should be out there! You know, I've never done it before, but I'm going to look into self-publishing. Maybe we can sell it on eBay."

And then my son went away for a while and "figured it out" while I sat at home trying not to think of the horror stories I had heard about writers who self-published—and had a basement full of unsold books. In the end, Mike and his company, mikeroweWORKS (MRW) Productions, were up to the task.

I felt quite the literary professional, sitting around my dining room table with my editor, Michele "Wojo" Wojciechowski, representatives from Zest Social Media Solutions (who were designing the layout and putting my book together), and Jade, all the way from MRW Productions in California. What fun, throwing out ideas about page numbering, chapter titles, pictures, and dozens of other details. Who knew there were so many decisions?

In my naivete, I'd assumed my work was finished. Silly me, not giving a thought to the title page, dedication, acknowledgments, foreword, and table of contents. Or even considering the inside front flap, inside back flap, biography, epilogue, and cover! We worked well into the evening that day, ironing out details while snacking on hummus, cheese and crackers, grapes, subs, and home-made cookies.

Printing ten thousand copies and putting them on eBay with no guarantee of a market was an enormous risk. But in 2018, *About My Mother* was published by MRW Productions.

When the printer sent me the first book off the line, I lifted it from the box as one might lift a newborn from a cradle. I embraced it—and cried. Not the same tears of rejection and despair I had shed through the years, but tears of gratitude and wonder. And though he won't admit it, so did my husband—before taking a hundred pictures of me holding our book in every pose imaginable (other than standing on my head) in every room of the house, even outdoors. I call it "our book" because John had read every word aloud to me so that I could hear it and get it right. Less than a month later, my son called with news that stopped my heart. Well, not really, or I'd be—you know.

"Mom, those ten thousand books we put on eBay...*they've all sold!*"

And that's when the real magic began. Publishers became aware of my book's popularity, read it, and came calling. Again, more heart-stopping news. "They want to publish your book, Mom! Big. Houses. Want. *Your* book! You have a decision to make."

Once I recovered from the shock, reality set in. "Oh, Mike," I said. "I don't know how to do this. You handle it, OK?" To say that I was suddenly embarrassed by the attention would be an accurate assessment. Suddenly, my book seemed small, inadequate, and unworthy of attention. It wasn't a page-turner. There wasn't even a narrative arc as such. Just because I had been compelled to write it was no guarantee it would have an audience. Would readers find the efficient, determined country girl who dedicated her life to her family, a sympathetic character? The woman who had seen her young husband's immense worth and potential—and orchestrated his career? Indeed, his very life? The woman who was determined that her two daughters would fulfill her own dreams?

Or would they see my mother through my young eyes? A bossy, domineering taskmaster who embarrassed me in my teens by dancing in the aisle at Memorial Stadium and shouting obscenities at umpires? What's more, my straightforward, simple style of writing precluded beautiful, flowing passages that one might want to read over and over. And Lord knows, there was no earth-shattering or groundbreaking content. It was just a growing-up story. Most of all, were publishers interested just because I was Mike Rowe's mother?

Mike sensed my insecurities. "Believe me, it's a mercenary business, Mom. Even if they did read it just because you're my mother, they wouldn't publish it if it wasn't good. It has warmth and humor, and a mother/daughter relationship people will relate to." Then, like a parent guiding an offspring along her professional journey, he said, "And now *you* need to choose a publisher *you* like, Mom—somebody you're comfortable with. Because you'll have a close working relationship."

Publishers from the very same houses that had rejected my earlier books traveled to Baltimore to meet me. They brought flowers and gifts and took me to lunch. As they made their pitches and detailed their plans for marketing and book tours, I fantasized about how I would go about rejecting the ones that didn't *measure up*. Maybe I'd tell them, "I'm sorry, but after careful consideration, your proposal just isn't the right fit for my needs at this moment. You see, my list is short. Maybe next time." Then I could add, "But don't give up; your work shows great promise ... good luck!" When I came home and told my husband about the publisher who had just offered me a three-book deal, he laughed. "Boy, if that isn't *the height of optimism*! They do know you're eighty, right?"

Mike and John and I discussed the publishers, their offers, their personalities, and the pros and cons of large versus small publishing houses. I chose Jonathan Merkh. Not just because he had seemed slightly nervous when he arrived at our condominium that hot August afternoon ... and reluctantly agreed to remove his sport coat and enjoy some lemonade and a piece of homemade applesauce cake. Publishers probably have limited opportunities to work with writers in their eighties—and for some reason, he brought out my maternal instincts. He was probably surprised to find me upright and chatty—and not drooling in my lemonade.

I went with Jonathan mostly because with twenty-five years of publishing experience under his belt, he had left his executive position at Simon & Schuster to start his own company, Forefront Books—though he still had a close association with Simon & Schuster, which would handle the distribution of my book. I would be Forefront's *first author*, just as Forefront would be my first book publisher. "*About My Mother*," Jonathan assured me, was a perfect fit for the nonfiction, inspirational memoirs that would be Forefront's focus.

The question I had was, would Jonathan still want to be my publisher after meeting me? That very evening my question was answered when Mary, Mike's partner and president of MRW, shared the email she had received from Jonathan. It was memorable for sure!

"*Love her!*...I'll have a proposal for you within twenty-four hours. Remember, time is of the essence...."

My new publisher made one demand of me. And I hated it!

Chapter 15

YOU'VE GOT TO BE KIDDING!

IN THE WORDS OF MY VETERAN PUBLISHER, "A SOCIAL media presence is an absolute *must* for an author in this day and age. That is, if you expect to sell books. And we do!"

"No way am I getting on Facebook!" I told my husband. "It's a colossal waste of time!" I'd heard it said many times, especially by people of my generation.

I knew that Jonathan was right, of course. Readers would get a sense of style and voice from my Facebook posts and want to read more—hopefully. That said, learning to navigate Facebook for this techno-challenged eighty-year-old was as complicated as writing a book. How embarrassing that millions of people use Facebook every day with ease, and I hadn't a clue how to begin.

Fortunately, MRW had the perfect solution: "People." One of my people is a woman named Shari who is not only savvy about social media but has the patience of a geriatric social worker. Really! Who knew that *counseling the elderly* was in her job description? And counsel, she did.

To say that I hated the process is an understatement. Posting two hundred words a couple of times a week on Facebook felt like feeding the beast. My page had an insatiable appetite not only for words, but for actual interesting, entertaining *content* for the couple of hundred people who initially followed me! Then there were the comments, many of which I responded to—which took valuable time away from writing my second book.

By the time *About My Mother* was launched, I had become a slightly more confident blogger. And as it turned out, my books and my Facebook page would have a symbiotic relationship. *About My Mother* made for convenient material for discussion on my blog, and some of my Facebook posts and comments made for interesting content in my second book, *About Your Father.* Shari continues to be a valuable resource when things fall apart. If I should click on "Post" and nothing happens, or my pictures are upside down and the "rotate" option isn't functioning, it's "Shari to the rescue." On one such occasion, the pictures were posted sideways for a half hour or so while I tried to figure it out. By the time I sent up an SOS to Shari, readers were commenting that their necks were getting stiff.

When writing the letter to Mike about losing my blue purse a year earlier, I had jokingly referred to his FB followers as "Your Little Facebook Friends." They (most of them) loved it, and the name *stuck*. My followers are also affectionately known as my LFBF.

<< ◆ >>

It was obvious even before my book launch that I had made the right choice in Jonathan Merkh. I knew it the day he called me while I was playing mah-jongg with some church friends. "Hi, Jonathan," I said. "I'm sorry, but I can't talk to you right now. I'm in the middle of a game of mah-jongg. I'll call you back in an hour." And he laughed. My publisher simply laughed. "OK," he said. "I'll wait for your call." I'd no sooner said goodbye when it hit me: considering all those years I had pursued publishers ... if someone had told me a year ago that I would blow off my publisher—for a game of mah-jongg—I'd have said they were crazy.

And who'd have thought that a publisher would personally accompany an author on her book tour? But that is exactly what he did. Perhaps because it was my first or maybe because of my age. Whatever. He was the perfect guide in New York City, leading my entourage safely from our hotel to television and radio studios and personal appearances. As dictated by tradition, my book was launched on a Tuesday. For two full days, my guardian angels and I rode from interview to interview in a big black car. Jonathan, Mike, Mary, and my John were beside me every step of the way.

There were live and taped television interviews, and radio and podcast interviews, one after the other. We met celebrities, and I learned firsthand the value of makeup artists—*magicians* who made this eighty-year-old woman look almost decent for the camera. On the second afternoon as we were leaving a book signing at the Fifth Avenue flagship Barnes & Noble, Jonathan asked, "Well, what do you think of your first book tour?"

"I feel like Cinderella at the ball," I told him.

"And the best is yet to come," he said, with an air of mystery. We climbed back into our car for a short ride to the Simon & Schuster headquarters in Rockefeller Center. When I saw the street sign "Avenue of the Americas," I felt a twinge but kept it to myself. How many times had I written that address on my manuscript submissions—and seen the same return address on the rejection letters from various big publishing houses—a lifetime ago.

We stepped from the car and followed Jonathan along the prestigious entrance corridor to the Simon & Schuster complex—stopping midway at a large, brightly lit showcase display. There, I saw dozens of copies of one book only: *About My Mother: True Stories of a Horse-Crazy Daughter and Her Baseball-Obsessed Mother,* by none other than Peggy Rowe. I wondered what other books had rested on those same shelves over the years—a humbling thought, for sure. John took my hand as he had the day we stood in awe at the rim of the Grand Canyon. Mike put his arm around my shoulder, and my publisher smiled proudly—as a parent might, watching his child survey Santa's gifts on Christmas morning.

There were photos, of course, but the rest of the afternoon is somewhat of a blur. The champagne reception at Simon & Schuster with staff, editors, and executives; the short speeches congratulating Jonathan on his "quick turnaround" of a book he had received a mere three months earlier; and me, for producing such a good read. I panicked when I realized I was expected to make a short, impromptu speech. I needn't have worried. I still remember my first two sentences.

Bold as brass and smiling, I said, "Thank you so much for all of this! And just so you know, I've decided to forgive each and every one of you for all of those rejection notices you've sent me through the years." There was good-natured laughter, and I felt pretty silly looking out at those fresh faces who were probably in elementary school when I had submitted my book manuscripts decades earlier.

There was a festive dinner at the hotel that evening with Mike, Jonathan, Mary, and me. John was tired and decided to heat up his leftovers from lunch in the microwave in our room. As the rest of us were perusing the dinner menu, John appeared at the table and provided the evening's entertainment.

"I've decided to join you," he said. "The microwave in our room is broken. The door won't stay shut. It flies open every time I set the timer."

"Where is it, Dad—this . . . microwave?" Mike asked. "Because my room doesn't have one."

"Neither does mine," said Mary.

"Well, that's another weird thing. It's inside the closet," John said, with a baffled look. "That's a funny place for a microwave."

"That's because it's not a microwave, Dad," Mike said, laughing. "You've been trying to heat up a sandwich in your *safe!*"

Nobody laughed harder than John.

After dinner, I posted a blog to my LFBF from my New York City hotel room:

Setting: *New York City. Barnes & Noble Flagship Store on 5th Avenue–for many years their largest store.*

Time: *4 PM—Tuesday, November 13th, 2018—the day of my book launch.*

Characters: *John Rowe and his author-wife, Peggy Rowe. A stranger named Leslie.*

Plot: *My entourage casually approaches the table at the front of the store. The one that's below the bold sign proclaiming: New Releases. There, we get some pictures of my books on display–while trying to appear cool. Then we meander to the Biography section for more photos.*

The manager sees us and brings a stack of books for me to sign. "Thank you for doing this," he says, applying stickers to the front covers that say, "Autographed." At this point, John steps away with one of my books and approaches an innocent shopper at a nearby table. He looks as though he's about to do a man-on-the-street interview.

"Oh no," I think, because with my husband, one never knows! Suddenly, he opens the book and begins reading aloud to this innocent shopper— this perfect stranger. I avert my eyes (because that's what I do in these situations) and continue signing the stack of books. When I finish and look up again, I'm face to face with the woman— and wondering if I should apologize.

"This is Leslie," John says. "Leslie, this is my wife, Peggy Rowe, the author of this book."

"Well, now I have to buy it," the woman says, taking the book from John. "I need to read the rest of that story you started. Would you sign it for me, Mrs. Rowe?" And that's how John sold my first book (possibly) in Barnes & Noble—on the very day it came out.

Thursday evening after arriving home, I wrote another short post:

"Cinderella has returned from her magical, whirl-wind, New York City book tour. I'm pleased to say that, not only does she have both of her slippers—she brought Prince Charming home with her."

Since that day, John has been known to my LFBF as *Prince Charming* (or PC). He's not crazy about the nickname. "It's a lot to live up to," he says. (So far, no problem.)

That weekend I did my first ever book event. It was held at my local library, and the night before I'd dreamed that I walked into a completely empty room. When I saw the packed auditorium, I might have teared up just a little. As it turned out, I was hardly nervous at all. You-know-who was on the front row videoing the action. Really—sometimes he takes my breath away! And my friend and editor, Michele, was on the back row making notes for me. Old friends and neighbors *and* an entire row of church friends, including my minister, were cheering me on. How could I help but succeed?

And then I went to bed and slept for a week.

In the end, this eighty-year-old woman who had never paid a bill, balanced a checkbook, or made financial decisions, happily turned over the business side of my late-in-life career to my son and MRW. There have been no regrets.

Shortly after my book hit shelves, another miracle occurred. It was a Saturday morning about ten o'clock when the phone rang. John answered it at the kitchen table on speaker. It was son Mike.

"Dad, what are you doing right now?"

"Your mother and I are having breakfast. I cooked the perfect omelet with ham and …."

"Dad … I want you to look at your wife. Are you looking at her?"

"Yes, Mike, she's right here beside me. What's this all about?"

"Dad! You are looking at a *New York Times best-selling author!!!*"

"*Get outta here!*"

Again, I might have teared up; old people do that a lot. And I might have screamed for joy, just a little, despite a miserable cold. Surely, I was dreaming.

The following morning, with my illness keeping me home from church, I had a visitor. My next-door neighbor, Jim, carrying copies of the *New York Times*, the *Wall Street Journal*, and the *Baltimore Sun*, and appearing every bit as excited as I, confirmed the full extent of Mike's news. Naturally, after calling family, I sat at my computer and shared the good news with my LFBF through some creative verse—the kind that rhymes.

Quoth My Neighbor

Once upon a Sunday dreary,
As I languished, weak and weary,
At the kitchen window of our
condo—2nd floor
Sipping tea and munching toast,
Watching him whom I love most,
Step into our car, and shut the door.
Off to church and Mickey Dee's,
Whilst I heave a mighty sneeze,
Bundled in my robe of gray velour.

Pondering life and lightly napping,
Suddenly I hear a tapping,
Someone gently rapping, rapping,
At my condo door.
Tis my neighbor with some news,

To wipe away my morning blues,
And fill my soul with happiness galore.

Seems my humble little tome,
Has found a temporary home,
On the *New York Times* best-seller list—
what's more…
There's *US News & World Report*,
Don't sell the *Wall Street Journal* short,
They're in agreement, that's great news,
for sure!

And then my neighbor said to me,
With a hint of merriment and glee,
As he turned and headed for my
chamber door.

"So when can we expect to see,
The next great masterpiece from thee?
It's been a month, what art thou waiting for?"
Thus quoth my neighbor evermore.

Peggy Rowe, 2018, with a special shout-out
to fellow Baltimorean Edgar Allen Poe…and
my dear neighbor Jim Durkin.

My next phone call was from Mike telling me that my little book—a story that was filled with hope—was now number one at Barnes & Noble—over Bob Woodward's mega book *Fear*. "Yep," Mike said. "Hope trumps fear."

Before long, I settled into a comfortable social media routine and discovered that almost anything can be material if written about in an interesting way. From recipes to after-church gatherings at McDonalds to the adventures of rubber duckies around the neighborhood, readers relate to and embrace our mundane lives. When my husband had hernia surgery and we kept track of his nighttime trips to the toilet by dropping pencils into the bathroom sink, readers followed with interest his nightly pencil count. When my soft-boiled egg exploded in the microwave, thousands of people shared their own exploding egg stories. Who knew? And when John made me a coffee table at the wood shop, my post went viral.

The writer in me pays attention to *everyone*. It's something I've learned from the experts over the years. I've written about our friends, neighbors, and family...as well as our minister, grocer, hairdresser, GP, GYN, dentist, dermatologist, urologist, cardiologist, electrician, and plumber—all with humor. Without exception, they have been willing subjects. My husband worries that people are going to see me approaching and clam up.

> John: *"You turn every conversation into an interview. People talk to you, and you turn around and write about them."*
> Me: *"But I change their names; I give them anonymity."*
> John: *"Hon! You include their pictures!"*
> Me: *"But only with their permission, and I always ask them first if they're wanted by the law ... or if they're in the witness protection program."*

What John says is true, and I've made an important discovery about my readers. They love it when I'm a tad naughty—without actually stepping over that line of decency. I recently included this passage in a blog. It's from an essay in my second book, *About Your Father*, and it's called "The Old Gray Pair." For my Facebook blog, I called the excerpt "Geriatric Erotica":

> *One evening after dinner, my husband and I were hugging in the kitchen when our visiting son wrapped his arms around us and lifted us off the floor saying, "You guys are adorable!" I wonder what he'd have said if he'd seen us at bedtime.*
>
> *"Do you have the stuff?" John asked me as I got into bed.*
>
> *"Of course," I said. "Here, you do me first."*
>
> *"Uh-uh. You know how you are; you get all steamy. You do me first."*
>
> *"All right, but you better hadn't fall asleep!" I warned him. I love to hear his groans of ecstasy as I do my thing.*
>
> *Nothing relieves my husband's itchy back like cortisone cream. And what he said about me is true. BenGay on my shoulders and neck can produce too much heat if he's not careful.*
>
> *John knows what I like.*

Life here at "the home" has provided a wealth of material. An audience favorite was my post about the elderly woman in the locker room. She stepped from the shower and passed in front of me on the way to her locker. Her front was covered with a towel, and I was shocked to see a slightly faded and sagging tattoo on her bottom—red, white, and blue with some writing.

Naturally, the inquisitive writer within me pointed to her bottom and asked, "Tell me about your tattoo." She looked confused, backed up to the mirror, and laughed. I joined her and read aloud, "Weis Markets—gas rewards." When we'd finished laughing, she explained, "After my shower, I spread a plastic grocery bag on the bench and sat down to dry my legs and feet."

As I said, material is everywhere.

≪ ◆ ≫

I've learned more about human nature in the past four years from my social media readers than in the past *eighty*-four years of life. People are hungry for something positive and uplifting. Something they can relate to, something that makes them laugh. During a time of turmoil and illness—with quarantine and life-changing uncertainty in nonstop news cycles—I have avoided controversial topics and continue to do so, even now.

Writing a book is a solitary pursuit with hours spent alone at a computer with little or no feedback. The comments written by my social media followers, whether they refer to a current short post or a story from one of my books, provide a wide range of views and even immediate gratification. Connecting with my readers reminds me who my audience is, which is an enormous advantage to any writer. Who'd have thought I would ever have a fan club? Had it not been for my LFBF, their acceptance, and their enthusiasm for the graphic nitty-gritty of everyday humor around us, I doubt I'd have had the courage to write and share the following *oh-so-true* stories.

"Maintenance 101: The Battle of the Bulge"

A fan once asked, "Mrs. Rowe, can you describe old age in three words?"

"Oh, that's easy," I said. "Patch, patch, patch." And it's true. Our bodies are like our old cars. It's all about maintenance. Your engine light comes on, and you hightail it to a garage. Some repairs are easy—in and out in a day. Others are more time-consuming and expensive—not to mention *painful.* To put it briefly, our body parts have a shelf life, which varies from person to person.

In 2019, my husband had what the doctor called "a little procedure." His inguinal hernia had been popping out at inconvenient times for the past several years, kind of like a nosey neighbor who sticks her head through the door, uninvited. You never knew when it might make an appearance. John could be in full stride and mid-sentence, when suddenly, the hernia would emerge through his abdominal wall, prompting him to reach down with both hands and push the nosey neighbor back through the door. He was like a walking Whac-A-Mole game, beating his hernia into submission.

When I made comments such as, "One of these days, you won't be able to shove that thing back in," he would say, "Give it a rest, Peg. You worry too much." And then one day my prediction came true, and my husband's bulge had to be dealt with by a surgeon.

Along with the repair of the hernia, John's longtime hydrocele was "corrected." As you may know, the hydrocele is a small sac of fluid in the scrotum. This one had been hanging around for way too long.

The surgery, an outpatient procedure, was not without side effects (or more accurately, *frontal* effects). I feel that I should post a message here, like those disclaimers on PBS warning of explicit content that may not be appropriate for all viewing audiences. It's usually followed by a show that has language, or sex, or violence. Consider yourself *forewarned.*

Late that night following the surgery, my husband and I were at home as the anesthesia was wearing off. He lifted the sheet, stared wide-eyed for a second, then screamed like a man engulfed in flames. "Peg! Come here! Quick!"

I pulled away the sheet and thought, "My Lord, what's an eggplant doing down there on his private parts?" I knew, of course, that it was my husband's scrotum, but only because of the position it occupied between his legs.

Knowing that John needed a calming influence, I did not gasp but, instead, said in a soothing voice, "Well, honey, Dr. Steele did say that you could expect some swelling and bruising. Remember?"

"*Some* swelling? *Some* bruising? There's a freaking eggplant between my legs!!!"

He was right—complete with a plump stem. "I'm calling 911," I said as my husband wobbled toward the bathroom, looking like a character from *March of the Penguins.*

"No way!" he yelled. "Do you really want an ambulance screeching in here at 2 a.m.?"

There are few secrets in a condominium community, especially when it comes to vehicles with flashing lights and screaming sirens. Many's the time we've stood at our kitchen window waiting to see who's being hauled through their front door like a piece of discarded furniture on dumpster day.

"It looks like that tall gentleman with a mustache," John might say. Or, "I think it's somebody heavy, with white hair," I'll speculate.

So I did what I always do when we have a medical crisis. I ran down to the first floor and knocked on our neighbor's door. Debbie is a retired nurse with a calm, professional demeanor. It was Debbie who helped the EMT crew maneuver my ninety-year-old mother onto a stretcher the night she fell and broke her hip. It was Debbie who loaned us a blood pressure kit when we had the flu, and an ankle wrap when our son sprained his foot. It was Debbie who made us a casserole when I broke my fifth metatarsal, and . . . You get the picture. So naturally, it was Debbie who came to our rescue in the middle of that fateful night.

Now wait a minute, you're probably thinking. *Do you mean to say that John actually shared his not-so-little problem with a neighbor? A female neighbor?*

I should probably mention here that John has had bouts of recurring bladder cancer over the past fifteen years or so. So he is no stranger to displaying his *intimate* body parts. There have been countless cystoscopies where his doctor and assistant introduce tools into the bladder to have a look around—through the obvious and only accessible route.

After that first procedure, my husband came home shaking his head and laughing. "You'll never guess what his pretty young assistant said when they finished."

"Umm . . . 'It has been my pleasure, Mr. Rowe'?" I said.

"She said, 'And now I'll give you some privacy while you get dressed, Mr. Rowe.' Can you believe that?"

So, yes, my husband has become somewhat desensitized over the years.

Well, God bless Debbie. She did not run screaming, or pass out, or even gasp when John lowered the sheet to reveal the vegetable of the day—with stem. Instead, she beheld the monstrosity between his legs and pronounced calmly but with authority, "Your surgeon needs to take a look at this . . . *right now.*"

Dr. Steele was delighted to get our call at 2:15 a.m.

"Mrs. Rowe, as you might remember, I offered to see your husband when we spoke this afternoon. And again, earlier this evening. He *declined*. Both times."

"I know and I'm sorry, Doctor, but my neighbor says it doesn't look normal."

"Your neighbor? So . . . your neighbor's on the case?"

That's when Debbie said, "Ask if we can send him a picture."

"Sure," the doctor said, stifling a yawn. "By all means, send me a picture of your husband's scrotum."

I took two photos—one from the top, and one from underneath while John elevated the "subject."

"Get good and close, hon. Make sure it's in focus. We want the color to pop! *And do not get my face in it!*"

I briefly pictured the image on a social media page with the caption: "Can You Identify This?"

"Hold on a minute!" Debbie said. "Before you hit 'Send,' make sure you have the right number."

I shuddered at the thought, imagining a scenario where an elderly insomniac is in bed watching a Hallmark movie. She gets a text. Who could it be at this late hour? There must be some kind of emergency. She pauses

Christmas Wishes and Mistletoe Kisses and glances at her phone, now bursting with geriatric pornography. The poor old dear would probably never close her eyes again.

"Well … it isn't pretty," the doctor said, "but I don't think it's gangrenous. If you want to be sure, though, you can go to the ER. What does your neighbor think?" I ignored the sarcasm, thanked him, and prepared for the drive to the hospital.

My husband's eyes were wide as his hands clenched the armrest and dashboard in the wee hours of that morning. I couldn't be sure if it was pain or fright. Cataracts and glaucoma make nighttime driving a challenge for me, but like I told John, "How important are those white lines when there's so little traffic? I can still see the road … sort of."

Five hours later, after multiple tests and scans in the ER, Dr. Steele made an appearance with a group of interns on morning rounds.

He had his smartphone out, and I was pretty sure he and the interns weren't gawking at the weather app as they huddled around the foot of my husband's bed. Our doctor was probably thinking, *Some people get pictures of grandkids on their phones.*

During the great unveiling, Dr. Steele said to the interns, "So have you guys ever seen *Dirty Jobs* with Mike Rowe? Well, guess what? These are his parents!"

He always introduces us that way. Don't get me wrong. We're proud of our son, but the *Dirty Jobs* humor loses its *punch* when your husband's scrotum is on full display … or, say, during a colonoscopy. It's a bit too *on the nose*, as it were.

Anyway, the test results were good, so after a thorough examination, we returned home midmorning where Debbie was waiting with a flexible ice wrap, ideal for the task at hand.

As the doctor predicted, the swelling and bruising gradually disappeared, and after weeks of stool softener and MiraLAX, I'm relieved to say that the unwelcome eggplant gradually withered away, and my husband's body parts returned to normal.

I admit to having selfish feelings about the repair of John's hernia. To be honest, I kind of miss it. Like the gopher in *Caddyshack,* that bulge had become a recurring character in my stories and social media posts, always good for a laugh. More than once when we were out walking, I would turn to John and ask, "What did you say, hon?" To which he would respond, "I didn't say anything."

It was his hernia talking, of course—the lead instrument in the one-man band my husband had become with a groaning bulge, backed up by the whistling hearing aids, a creaking foot brace, and the occasional fanfare from the brass section, always there to keep the tempo peppy. Enough said about that.

Of course, I'm relieved that John had the "little procedure" and is back to good health. That said, we're still not eating eggplant, and I've noticed that John continues to have trouble looking our neighbor Debbie in the eye. As for her ice wrap, I washed it thoroughly and returned it, but what are the odds she'll ever use it again?

≪ ◆ ≫

Bulges in the elderly are as common as forgetfulness and mobility issues. I was doing a signing in a bookstore when a jolly, middle-aged woman approached and handed me a copy of my book, saying, "Oh Mrs. Rowe, you make old age seem like such fun. I'm actually looking forward to it."

I wanted to say to her, "Seriously? Pull up a chair, honey. I have a little story for you."

"Material Girls"

My particular bulge was as personal as my husband's. Simply put, after spending eighty-two years in a sheltered, confined environment, my bladder became curious about the outside world. So, anxious for a glimpse of the good life, she headed south. As the expression goes, "After seeing Gay Paree, it was impossible to keep her down on the farm," or should I say, *up in the north pasture.*

My GYN assured me that prolapse is common. "Fifty percent of women over the age of fifty experience it." She told me this as I was on the table with my feet in the air . . . a captive audience, so to speak. "It's usually the result of gravity and childbirth. Look at it this way," she said. "It's one more reason to make your children feel guilty."

I made a mental note to remember that one. It might come in handy some time. Not that I would dream of using it.

It was at this point in our relationship that the middle-aged doctor and I began chatting personally. When I told her that I was a writer of mostly humor, she shared with me that she moonlights as a stand-up comic.

"Really?" I said. I would never have guessed; she looked reserved and kind of serene—not traits one normally associates with stand-up comics. Plus the fact that she had not once used profanity.

"Well, you certainly have some great material!" I said, imagining her typical day looking at women's bottoms.

There was a twinkle in her eye when she said, "You could be the subject of my next routine," which, of course, had already occurred to me. She quickly added, "Naturally, I don't use names or pictures," and laughed.

"That's very reassuring," I said, and reminded her of a recent news story about a doctor who had photographed patients without their knowledge.

"No cameras," she said, looking around the room and laughing. "Not even in the ceiling."

She finished her examination and explained that I had three options: I could live with the prolapse; I could schedule surgery, which she described in detail; or I could try a pessary. Apparently, many women have success with the plastic ring-like device which, when fitted correctly, holds things in place.

I grimaced. "Ooh…."

"Think of it as a piece of jewelry," she said. "They come in sizes 2–7. I would use a size 3 on you. We can always make adjustments."

"A size 3? Really?" I have to admit, I was flattered and began to consider the possibilities. I could brag that I was wearing a ladylike size 3—like those women who brag about their petite size 8 dresses. I couldn't wait to tell my husband.

So I opted to avoid surgery and go with the pes…"jewelry."

This meant returning to the office from time to time for some scheduled "maintenance," kind of like my husband takes the car in for a thousand-mile check-up—oil change or grease job. But overall, I treated my pessary like jewelry, taking her to church, and the grocery store, and the theater....

Alas, there were size adjustments down the road—always larger, unfortunately. But it's just a number, right? And who cares? Let's just say I didn't do any bragging. And to the doctor's credit—not once did she refer to it as the Hula Hoop. I eventually opted for the surgery. My self-esteem couldn't take any more.

At my surgical follow-up appointment, my doctor was looking through the speculum at her handiwork when she smiled and said one word: "Beautiful!" To which I responded, "You really have to get out more!"

We *girls* both laughed—pleased with our "new material."

<< ◆ >>

In recent years, the children have made "assessment visits" where they've considered our needs and well-being. Not that they would say as much, but we can tell. From advising us on the purchase of a television and carrying it in from the car, to hanging dozens of pictures in our new residence, to making trips to Goodwill and the dump to dispose of our unwanted items. Sometimes their interest in our well-being is a mixed blessing.

"Don't Shoot Your Eye Out!"

"Now what the heck is this?" my husband said as he came into our condo with a big box. He was carrying it well away from his body as though it might contain a poisonous snake. "We didn't order anything from Amazon."

We're not the kind of people who order things online. We shop the old-fashioned way.

I still remember John's expression when he opened the box with a mixture of confusion and wonder. "What the ...? Who would be sending us an *Adventure Force Tactical Strike Sentry X2 Ball Blaster?*"

"Oh no!" I said, stepping back. "*It's a machine gun!* Don't touch it, John!"

"Don't be silly! It's not a machine gun. It's a ... *pistol;* a pistol that shoots Nerf balls!" His eyes sparkled like a kid's on Christmas morning.

"Well don't take it out of the box!" I yelled. "We have to send it right back! It's a mistake."

And then we saw the card from our son. This was no mistake....

***

There's nothing funny about hearing loss. My husband faced his square on ... with denial. There was nothing wrong with *his* hearing. It was *my* fault I mumbled. "You have to enunciate," he told me. When I raised my voice in order to be heard, I was accused of being angry and impatient.

After I threatened to register us for a course in signing for the deaf, he agreed to see an audiologist and got his first pair of hearing aids. Things improved a little, but our television continued to blast away, causing the lampshades and living room windows to vibrate. John denied any connection between the vibrating and his hearing, so I told him there was a petition being circulated in our building about the noise pollution from our TV. So he did some research and discovered TV Ears, a simple Bluetooth wireless headset that allows him to hear the television at a reasonable volume and our neighbors and me to remove our earplugs. The downside, of course, is that when he's wearing the TV Ears, conversation between us is impossible. He hears only the television.

Weeks later, as luck would have it, son Mike came to visit, observed our problem, and surprised us with a *dry erase board*—complete with markers and erasers.

Such a clever idea! I could sit on the sofa, scribble my comments, and hold up the board. John, sitting in his blue lounger six feet away had only to read it and react. Voilà!

There was just one problem—getting his attention. I screamed! I waved a towel in the air! I threw a pillow at him (and hit the lamp). By the time he looked up, the action had moved on, and my comment was irrelevant. I texted Mike and told him about my dilemma.

And that's when the package arrived from Amazon. I read the enclosed card:

> *Hey Mom. Here's the perfect way for you to get Dad's attention while he's using his TV Ears. Just load the gun ... shoot ... and bounce a Nerf ball off his leg. Then hold up the message board. PS: Don't shoot your eye out! Mike*

Before I knew what was happening, my husband had unwrapped the weapon, loaded it, and was shooting random targets around the living room with a crazed gleam in his eye. First, our family photograph hanging on the wall, then the thermostat, then the ceiling fan. He was eyeing the dining room fixture when *Midsomer Murders* came on PBS.

It was a typical evening in the Rowe house with John ensconced in his blue leather recliner, TV Ears in, and me on the sofa with a cup of decaf, dry erase board—and my Adventure Force Tactical Strike pistol, fully loaded with six rounds of Nerf ammo.

What could possibly go wrong?

Well, let me tell you.

A few minutes into the show, I wrote the name of the murderer on the board, laid it down, picked up my pistol, and shot my husband's glasses clear off his face. Before I knew what I was doing, I'd squeezed off another round, this time hitting a lower target. Let's just say they don't call this the "Ball Blaster" for nothing. John was not pleased! As luck would have it, he isn't a violent man.

Anyway, they're always saying that the most dangerous firearms are possessed by people who don't know how to use them. So yesterday morning, I stood in the sunroom and did some target practice—under my husband's tutelage, of course. Unfortunately, I was in front of the big window as a passerby glanced up and saw somebody with a gun in a threatening pose. She called the building captain (instead of the police, thank heaven). What a mess!

We had to get rid of the gun when we moved into "the home." Apparently, there are rules about old people and machine guns. But that's okay. Things are simpler nowadays. My husband and I sit side by side on the sofa when we watch TV. All I have to do is lean over, take his earpiece out, and yell.

Chapter 16

A MEMOIR, SHE WROTE

BEING A FIRST-TIME AUTHOR GAVE NEW PURPOSE TO my outings. It was impossible, for instance, to pass our library without stopping in to visit the Memoir/ Biography section—kind of like one might stop to visit a favorite friend. I've even been known to replace the book currently on the display stand with my own. Sometimes an accomplice acts as a lookout—an elderly, innocent looking gentleman. One day I was visiting a library outside of my neighborhood and checked on my book. It was nowhere to be found, so I played it cool and asked the librarian if they carried *About My Mother* by Peggy Rowe. "Could it be on display in another area...?" I suggested. She checked her computer.

"I'm afraid all of our copies are out, and there are three people ahead of you," she said. "Do you want me to put it on hold for you, Mrs. Rowe?" I might have turned the shade of Ralphie's bunny outfit in *The Christmas Story* and said something like "Busted!" We had a good laugh together before she said, "By the way, it was a fun read!" Don't you just love librarians?

And bookstores—don't get me started! I had no shame in rearranging displays. I had learned early on not to take my book from the shelf and peruse. I invariably wanted to make changes. "Oh," I'd say to myself, "I should have said that differently. I wish I could do it over." Truth is, I could still be tweaking the stories in my first book— four years after publishing. But as all writers know, there comes a time when you must say good-bye and kick your literary fledgling from the nest.

It was mid-December when my daughter-in-law, Marjie, texted me with some "Before" and "After" pictures of the book table in her South Florida Walmart. The first picture showed two copies of my book partially obscured on the bottom shelf. In the second photograph, after Marjie's "rearranging," my books appeared on the top shelf proudly looking out at shoppers. A third picture, taken an hour later following Marjie's Christmas shopping, showed an empty space on the top shelf where my books had been—*prior to selling*! It occurred to me that having a large family scattered about could be advantageous indeed for an author.

"Me Too"—Not

I envy authors who have the good fortune to enjoy a career in their prime. Like those women who present at conferences, standing at the podium in a pretty little sun dress that accentuates their slim waist and shows off their shapely calves. For me, the "sundress ship" sailed during the Reagan administration; the more I cover up now, the more presentable I look. My pretty little outfit these days consists of black slacks and a loose-fitting top. At the age of eighty-four, I'm bullish on comfort and walking to the podium without limping. My only nod to fashion would be the laces in my tennis shoes that match my top.

Another downside to having your career take off when you're old is the whole energy thing. I recently listened to an interview with sixty-five-year-old author David Sedaris. He was on a *sixty-city* book tour in something like twenty days. As I mentioned earlier, I spent two days on a New York City book tour, came home, and slept for a week.

I used to worry about not being able to recall words or names while speaking. But I've learned that if you're up front with audiences, they cut you some slack. I was doing a Q&A at a library when I couldn't think of a word. So I pointed to my head and fessed up—saying something like "old brains . . . ." Someone called out, "What does the word mean?"

"Well," I said, "it's a story that someone recorded for you to listen to on your smartphone while you're out walking . . . ."

An enthusiastic voice from the back shouted "podcast!" There was laughter, so a little later I pretended to struggle for another word until someone came to my rescue—a kind of interactive charades. They loved it. Audiences remind me of the classes from my substituting days. No, they don't throw things or fight, and nobody has called out, "I don't have to listen to you; you're just a substitute!" But a speaker does get a sense early on if an audience is going to be fun. If so, and I'm at a podium for an hour or more, I might do some bends and stretches to avoid blood clots and frozen joints. They're fully on board; some might even join me. I might also share with them that I have a two-hour bladder. "But don't you worry," I say. "I came prepared." Yes, I've come a long way from that aged greenhorn, but I still marvel at a full audience.

There are definite advantages to a late-in-life career. For one, I can say with certainty that my work never interfered with my maternal responsibilities. Child Protective Services did not once pay me a visit or charge me with neglect. Erma Bombeck talked about her children slipping notes under the door while she was hard at work in her home office. Notes that claimed the house was on fire . . . or that the kid was being murdered by a sibling. Romance author Nora Roberts had what she calls "the fire and blood rule" when she was writing at home with two young sons. "Unless it's fire or blood, don't bother me!" Our three sons were in their fifties when my writing career took off. Fire, blood, and sibling violence were never issues outside of my office door. The only character intruding into my workspace has been an old man who lovingly sets my breakfast on a table beside me while admonishing, "Now eat while it's hot!"

Another advantage of being a late bloomer is that I haven't been part of the #MeToo movement. I didn't have to sleep my way to a publishing contract. And I can honestly say there has been no sexual harassment in my career—not by publishers, editors, book distributers, interviewers, or event organizers. Nope. Never. Zilch. Not one lousy time. If and when it should happen, I'm sure Prince Charming will handle it (as soon as he stops laughing).

"Blessed Is the Writer ... for She Shall Inherit the Truth"

If I have learned anything from writing, it is that nothing reveals *the big picture* quite like "telling the story." I had always thought of my mother as controlling—forcing me to go to church and Girl Scouts, wear dresses, take piano lessons, listen to opera, do my homework. She was a dictator devoted to molding her girls into refined young ladies and models of perfection who would reflect well on her—despite *their* desires. But in writing the stories for my book, I understood her motivation: her true nature was revealed. Instead of a nosey, prying mother, I saw a protective mother shielding her daughters from unwholesome relationships and environments. Even her disapproval of my husband-to-be was understandable. Fortunately, she backed down and never regretted it.

Reliving my childhood trip to the pony roundup in Chincoteague, Virginia, was more than an eye-opener. It gave me an appreciation for the busy mother and office manager who dropped everything, drove hundreds of miles to a strange town, and slept for two nights in a mosquito-infested station wagon in a parking lot. All so that her horse-crazed ten-year-old daughter might stare at ponies ... touch them ... smell them ... dream ... and store up a lifetime of memories.

Instead of the embarrassment I had felt seventy years earlier, writing about it allowed me to look back and laugh at my mother's desperate, dramatic performance before a mercenary motel manager who had tried to charge us seventy dollars a night—in 1948. "Shame on you for taking advantage of a mother and child!" she admonished. "I have a good mind to report you!" This, as I looked down at my cowboy boots and backed through the door onto the sidewalk.

Later, her performance in the firehouse was thoroughly persuasive as she clutched me to her side. There might have been a slight "catch" in her voice when she told the fire chief about our desperate situation and the merciless motel operator. He looked at the two weary travelers who had no place to spend the night, and, like the innkeeper in Bethlehem, took pity on us. Not only were we allowed to park directly in front of the firehouse for two nights, we had lavatory privileges *and* all the donuts we could eat.

My mother's most dramatic performance during that trip took place on the drive home when the policeman pulled us over for speeding. And really, it was Oscar-worthy.

Mom: (rolling down her window), "What is
        it, officer? Is there something wrong with
        my car?"
Officer: "Yes, ma'am. It was going too fast. Your
        license and registration, please."

Mom: "Me, speeding? You're mistaken. I've been
        driving since I was twelve. I've never even
        been pulled over."

Officer: "License and registration, please."

Mom: (breathless and coughing with her hand over
        her heart), "I don't feel very well ... this has
        never happened before."

Officer: (as I handed him an envelope from the
        glove compartment and slid lower in my seat),
        "You'll be alright, ma'am ...."

Mom: (rubbing the left side of her chest), "Are you
        sure about this, officer, because I've never ...."

Officer: (writing on a pad), "I'm sure, Mrs. Knobel.
        I'll just give you a warning this time, but you
        need to slow down; you have precious cargo."

A scene that was totally devoid of humor at the time
became clear when I wrote that chapter for my book.
What a wonderful aid is the memoir—to help us understand people, and behavior, and events. Even when they
happened seventy years ago.

"Blessed Is the Humorist ...
for She Will Live with Laughter"

When a woman stopped me in the grocery store and said,
"Oh, Mrs. Rowe, I can so relate to your writing. You and I
are just alike! Gray hair, wrinkles ... and I've put on some
extra pounds around the middle just like you," I saw the
humor and was able to laugh (instead of slinging a jar of
pickled beets at her).

Then there was the lady who compared my writing
to comfort food. "It puts me to sleep," she told me. I had

to laugh, but just as I was thinking *Boy, does this woman know how to give a compliment or what?* she continued. "You see, I keep your books on my bedside table. When I've had a terrible day and can't stop worrying, I read a chapter or two. My troubles melt away, and I'm asleep in no time. Please don't stop writing, Mrs. Rowe."

Even the occasional dark humor on my social media page makes me laugh. "Oh, Mrs. Rowe, this post was so funny, I nearly rolled off my hospital bed laughing."

I wasn't quite sure how to react to the young woman who touched my arm and said, "Mrs. Rowe, you are my dead grandmother all over!" So I simply smiled and tried to look pleased (and made a mental note to jot this one down). Then she went on to extol her grandmother's virtues and tell me how much of an influence she had been in her own life. "I loved her so much!" she said, eyes brimming. And then she asked me to sign two copies of my book. I've decided that being compared to dead relatives can be the ultimate compliment.

We were in the midst of the coronavirus shutdown when my second book hit the shelves (metaphorically speaking), so I wasn't able to go on a book tour. Instead, there were telephone and Zoom interviews. One day, there were as many as ten—where I answered some of the same questions over and over. My answers are always earnest, of course, but from time to time I have to admit...I fantasize about shaking things up. Just a little...

> Interviewer: "Peggy, in a time when the divorce rate is 40 to 50 percent, why do you think you and John have been able to stay together for sixty years?"

Me: "That's simple. Early on, neither one of us
        wanted custody of three boys. In later years,
        neither one of us has the energy to move out."
Interviewer: (Wide-eyed and clearing his throat),
        "I see, well, um … how do you and your
        husband spend your time during this
        quarantine?"
Me: "Uh—you mean when we're not fighting?"
Interviewer: (Nervous laughter …)
Me: John stays busy with his Internet porn sites.
        And I enjoy looking through the neighbors'
        windows with binoculars."

One of these days I'm going to give it a try.

≪ ◆ ≫

My childhood passion was horses, and my dream was to
be a professional rider and trainer. My mother helped
me to adjust that dream when I was in my teens. "Peggy,"
she said, "you have to be realistic. You need a career!
Horses are your *hobby*! They're not an appropriate
career for a young woman. Be a teacher. You were a fine
Sunday School teacher. And I've watched you teaching
children to ride. You're good with them; they love you."
Sometimes it's worth listening to our mothers.

When I became an adult, I used writing in my
teaching, and before long, it was my passion. It filled my
head and eventually my days, and I dreamed of being
an author and publishing books. Friends in my critique
group helped me to adjust that dream, and as a result, I

wrote shorter pieces—articles, stories, and essays that were easier to get published than a book.

Today I call myself a writer not because my name is on two *New York Times* best-seller lists, but because the people I have cared for most in this world have appreciated and benefitted from my modest works. My parents and sister, my husband and children, my friends and neighbors ... Their pride in my accomplishments has helped to keep my passion alive. The rest is icing on the cake. Or as my husband would say, "The pepperoni on the pizza." When my granddaughters, now in their thirties, recently recalled my first book that I shared with them all those years ago, I was speechless. That they would remember the plot and characters in such vivid detail left me humbled and grateful. Who knows? Maybe I'll open that drawer one of these days ....

And now, at the risk of sounding way too earnest, which I try to avoid like those lofty phrases, I must tell you: this book will not teach anyone how to write or how to get a book published. I'm far from an expert on either. I'm certainly not here to encourage readers to follow their dream, because sometimes dreams are unrealistic and need to be adjusted or deferred. Think of me as one of those folks by the side of the road who offers sustenance to those passionate marathon runners and cheers them on along their journey. Because who doesn't need someone to cheer them on—no matter what their passion may be? My all-time favorite quote is one attributed to Albert Schweitzer: "In everyone's life, at some time, our inner fire goes out. It is then burst into flame by an encounter with another human being."

John and I lived next door to my parents for most of our married life—which was, oddly enough, a good thing. I was visiting my mother one day when I looked around and saw her old Singer treadle sewing machine in the corner. She had made all of our clothes, as well as draperies, slipcovers, tablecloths, aprons, and Halloween costumes on that old machine.

"Oh Mom," I said, "you're eighty-five years old. You don't need to sew anymore. We can get rid of that old thing." I know—quite possibly the most insensitive words I've ever spoken.

She looked at me as though my hair were engulfed in flames. "Why would I want to do that, Peggy? I could still create my greatest masterpiece."

I wrote three books after the age of eighty—after a sixty-year journey with detours, disappointment, and doubt, along with some magnificent scenery. I've followed my passion throughout my adult life ... because I didn't have a choice. I simply don't know how *not* to.

Would that my story could inspire someone else. Remember, we might still create our greatest masterpiece.

ACKNOWLEDGMENTS

WITH SPECIAL THANKS TO:
My loving and supportive family . . . who have been known to read the words I write . . . and who claim to enjoy them.

Son Mike, who shares my passion, and without whom my writing journey would have been quite different.

Jaime Buckley, illustrator, for his clever cover design—as well as other chapter drawings.

My friends at mikeroweWORKS, who make my life easier—Mary, Jade, Chuck, Shari, Lara, and Libby.

Editors Lisa Stilwell and Billie Brownell, who helped to make this a real book.

Jonathan Merkh, Jennifer Gingerich, and the rest at Forefront Books, my publisher of choice.

My friend and first reader, Michele "Wojo" Wojciechowski, who always offers me good advice.

All of the people who read my books—and my hundreds of thousands of Little Facebook Friends.

ABOUT THE AUTHOR

PEGGY ROWE LIVES IN Baltimore, Maryland, with John, her husband of sixty-one years. Both educators, they raised three sons. Peggy has been writing for most of her adult life and has two *New York Times* best-sellers to her credit—both of which were published after the age of eighty. Now eighty-four, she is living the good life in a retirement community, where material abounds. Peggy continues to write every day of her life—preferably without wearing jewelry or a bra.

AVAILABLE FROM PEGGY ROWE